Loving My Lot

I've become addicted after only first visiting (*Loving My Lot*) after a friend was kind enough to share it on Facebook. You always speak such brutal truths and meet me where I am.

Kelli
Blog Follower

Your blog is one of my absolute favorites on the internet, not because you are the most practical or because you post the most, but because you speak to my heart about the season I am in and remind me of God's truth in and for it.

Courtney
Blog Follower

I have been reading what Jeanne Harrison writes since she first made her writing public. By her personal cross cultural experience and her education, she is well equipped to understand many of the challenges we face in today's world. Her strong commitment to Christ and her ability to handle the Word of God effectively make what she writes well worth reading. She is both profound and playful as her personality shines through in her writing. I often share something she writes with my friends and family.

Anne Wenger
Bridges International, Cru Staff Member

I found your blog today on Facebook...and I feel like I'm reading my own heart! Thanks for sharing.

Dana Hemminger
Author of *Reflections from Holland*

I'm a recent follower of your blog and have stayed up many nights lately pouring over your old posts. I so appreciate your honesty and openness. God has spoken to my heart through so many of your posts...I think it is great that you tackle some of the more "unpopular" subjects as well.

Maggie
Blog Follower

Jeanne's stories about being a mother and wife really speak to me. She writes with an honesty and truth that is refreshing and brings a Christian perspective to the many joys and struggles we face each day.

Vicki Sarajedini
Associate Professor of Astronomy, University of Florida

God has used your blog posts to make a significant difference in my life, and I am only one person but I'm being used to share with many.

Geneve
Blog Follower

Thank you for being used by him through this blog. It is one of my favorite to read...not because you are glorified, but because Jesus shines through brightly in every post.

Emily
Blog Follower

Loving My Lot

A Young Mom's Journey to Contentment

Jeanne Harrison

ISBN: 1508541744
ISBN 13: 9781508541745

Dedication

To Aubrey, Heidi, and Lila. One day I will give you this book, and with it, a window into my heart and my journey as your mom.

Table of Contents

Introduction xiii
WIFE 1
Two Different Men 3
What The Young Can Teach The Old About Love 7
Romancing a Guy 11
The Marriage Conversation You Ought to Have 15
Do You Ever Worry You'll Fall Out of Love? 19
Two Different Dances 23

MOM 25
The Rollercoaster 27
How a Baby Changes Your Life 31
Freedom from Fearful Parenting 37
What Kids Really Want 41
3 Ways to Raise a Pharisee 45
Assessing the Princess Obsession 49
5 Reasons I Fear Standing Up to My Kids 53
When Mom Just Needs a Good Cry 57
Raising Pure Kids in an Impure World 61
It's Okay to Admit It's Hard 65
The Mom Who Lies 67
How Mama Bear Hurts Her Family 71

Why the Vaccination Debate is So Nasty (And Why It Ought Not Be) 75
Secrets of a Sinful Mom 79
Peanut Butter Princess 81
Can You Really Raise a Child with an Unbiased Worldview? 83
Why Having More Babies Isn't as Crazy as You May Think 87
Mom vs. Mom: The War I Didn't See Coming 91

HOMEMAKER **95**
Running a Home While Running on Empty 97
The House that Cleans Itself 101
Eating to Honor God 105
8 Ways to Cultivate a More Restful Home 109
How Much Should a Mom Minister Outside the Home? 113
When Homemaking Becomes Idolatrous 117

WOMAN **121**
Guilt-Free Womanhood 123
The Woman I Wish I Could Be 127
Dangerous Daydreams 131
To Those Battling Biblical Womanhood 133
Innocent Envy 137
Why Women Wander 141
What I Want My Daughters to Know about Biblical Womanhood 143
Here's to the Woman Inside the Mom 147

CHILD **151**
The Master's {Violent} Mercy 153
The Things in My Life I Don't Like 155
On Leaving a Legacy 159

3 Things to Tell Yourself When Others Prosper While You Suffer. . . . 163
If Only Everyone Could Just Like Me. 167
When All You Can Do Is Wait. 169
Getting Real about the Girl Behind the Grin 173
Is There Such a Thing as Calling? 177
When Life Disappoints 181
An Ode to My Twenties. 185

Introduction

If you've ever had an entire bowl of oatmeal spilled in your lap (and worn the same pants anyway), or caught your toddler stark naked in the front yard teaching the dog how to pee in the grass, then maybe your current "lot in life" is similar to mine. Five years ago I packed up a beloved career to become a bona fide stay-at-home-mom. Never once have I regretted the decision. Yet despite my love for family and biblical living, three years ago I found myself ready to toss in the towel.

I could not reconcile the attractive ideals of biblical womanhood with the mundane realities of daily living. I felt like a ping pong ball ricocheting between guilt and entitlement: "I should be a better homemaker, more organized, better at training my children in godliness, more joyful in serving my husband…but what about *me*? What about *my* ambitions? *My* passions?" I thought of all the lesson plans I had carefully crafted as a teacher, all the praise I received for my efforts, all the ideas and dreams I'd nursed through adolescence…and here I knelt picking up the same toys in the same play room again… and again…and again.

Discontentment. It began to consume me.

It was in the midst of a particularly emotional gripe-fest with God that He directed me to a passage in Ecclesiastes. After condemning the "grievous evil" of a father who lost his son's inheritance and as a result had nothing to show for all his toil, the author goes on to write:

> Behold, what I have seen to be good and fitting is to eat and drink and *find enjoyment in all the toil* with which one toils under the sun the few days of his life that God has given him, *for this is his lot.*"[1]

The passage cut me to the heart. I had structured my toil, tried to become efficient in my toil, read books about my toil, but failed to find *enjoyment* in my toil. A few days later, I sat down at the kitchen table and did something I'd never done before. I created a blog. My brother had challenged me to blog for a while, but I thought it was a cheap substitute for my true ambition to write a book. But that day I was desperate for an outlet and sick of being too afraid to try something new.

Three years later, through this little blog, God has allowed me to have a voice in over 160 countries around the world. He's taken the broken bits of my journey and used them to speak into the lives of hundreds of thousands of people. Not because I'm so great, but because *He* is.

For months I meant to return to my ambition of writing a book, until one day I finally realized, I already have. Over the course of three years, I've penned thousands of words from the "trenches" of child-rearing, homemaking, and marriage. All that was left was to compile it.

The book you hold in your hands is a testimony of God's boundless grace. As a writer, the greatest joy is simply to be *read.* To produce something from your heart that touches something in another person's heart. That is my prayer for this book. I pray God would use it to touch you in real and powerful ways, so that together we may wrap both arms around the "lot" that is ours—the beautiful, painful, and at times downright disgusting! May this book be a simple way to celebrate our lot, indeed to love it.

Wife

"THERE IS NO CHARM EQUAL TO TENDERNESS OF HEART."

Jane Austen, *Emma*

Two Different Men

When I was but a youthful girl
Of four and seventeen,
I chanced upon two different men,
Whose natures were unseen.

One was handsome, tall, and dark,
With gallantry to spare,
He swept me off my feeble feet,
And made me twice as fair.

I came to know him by a word,
As we dined and danced,
For while he brought the stars to life,
I called him sweet ***Romance****.*

The other man was odd to me,
For he never left my side,
Though often I was known to gripe,
And roll my eyes and chide.

He did not lure with mystery,
Pour gifts upon my greed,
In fact at times he grew so dull
I scarcely paid him heed.

But as the days gave birth to years,
My skin came loose and gray,
And when I searched for my Romance,
He'd wandered far away.

I trembled in my lonely bed
With sickness and with fear.
"Do not cry," a soft voice said,
"I am ever near."

The other man stroked my face
And dried my weathered nose,
He brushed my hair with shaky hands,
He gently held me close.

"Where is the one who stole my heart,
Fierce and young and brave?
Why would he arise and leave
An old man in his place?"

With wrinkled lips he smiled and said,
"We've always been the same,
Both he and I were but one man
Resolved, your heart to claim.

He was grand and I was small,
When first we caught your whim,
And though I grew from day to day,
You always preferred him.

But now, my dear, as dusk draws near,
I have grown so vast,
That though he was the first to win,
It's me who'll be the last."

I held his face between my hands,
I cried into his tears,
Until his old familiar touch,
Had swept away the years.

At last I knew there was one thing
That I could be sure of:
And so I whispered in his ear,
"Then I shall call thee ***Love****."*

What The Young Can Teach The Old About Love

In the summer of 2005, Hurricane Katrina struck Louisiana, Lance Armstrong retired, and Clint Harrison asked me to marry him. I was twenty years old, and if you'd given me wings I'd have sailed straight to the moon. I'd like to think I took off the rose-colored glasses every now and then by reading marriage books and talking to wiser women, but the truth is, everything was tinged with Tinkerbell-like optimism. Sprinkled with pixie dust and all the tenderest hopes of my heart.

Once while we were engaged, we stole away into the woods by our college campus. It was the perfect fall day, and Clint (filled with his usual supply of boundless energy) told wild stories, chased me through the leaves, and laughed like a kid. And then I saw them. Each one of our future children...running around his legs, jumping on his back, squealing in the autumn air. It was one of the happiest moments of my life. A moment when I knew I was about to begin a beautiful adventure, the one I'd been waiting for.

I thought about that girl today. The one standing in the woods with a ring on her finger and stars in her eyes. I couldn't help but wonder how she would feel if she could see me now, nearly ten years later. Would she be proud of the woman I've become? Or disappointed? Would she look at my life and smile? Or frown? I've always thought I could teach that girl a lot if I owned a time machine. I would teach her that in the adventure of being a wife and mom, sometimes you look more like the wicked step-mother than the gracious queen. Sometimes the palace smells like the stable, and the prince makes you want to joust instead of dance. I would teach her that embracing boredom is brave and chasing fairytales is foolish. That the princesses of perfection and performance are actually the enemies, and the monsters of suffering and difficulty are the friends you must learn to love.

I would teach her all these things, and I imagine she'd be better for it. But today for the first time I wondered, if I shut my older and wiser mouth for just a second, what might *she* teach me?

Might she remind me how long we waited to be loved by a man, and how perhaps those dirty socks by the front door really weren't worth the ugly words? Would she remind me that we once held baby dolls in our arms and longed for the day when they would be real? Yes, I think she would.

I think she would tell me there's a fine line between "growing realistic" and growing cynical. And that irritation—or endearment—are choices we make every day. I think if that girl from the woods could see me now, she'd tell me to open my eyes. To realize I'm rich in all the ways I've always hoped to be, save one. I am poor in gratitude. And as a result, my heart may be older and wiser, but it is also harder.

So you want to know the first thing I am choosing to be grateful for today? Amid the clutter and crying and crusty cereal in the sink, today I am thankful for that girl. That young, naive girl...with the soft and tender heart. And I am praying that I welcome a little more of her back into my life every day.

Romancing a Guy

I have a theory that men desire romance just as much as women. I think they just define it differently. At least that's what I'm beginning to think as Valentine's Day rapidly approaches and I find myself quietly studying my husband. *What would* he *find romantic?* I already know the answer is not endless conversation or a sparkling toilet. Those things speak to his heart about as much as a power drill on my birthday would speak to mine. But that doesn't mean he has no need for romance.

After all, you don't have to be female to long for someone to know you, or to be delighted that someone has discovered you. To romance someone is to capture his affection by speaking in a language that touches him. It is to "see" inside of him and openly demonstrate that what you've seen is lovely. I don't think there's a manly man in the world who doesn't desire that to some degree. So...*how do you romance a man?* Obviously, all men are different, but at the risk of being written off, I am going to make three sweeping generalizations that I think hold true for *most* men.

Listen to him.

Even when it's boring. This is critical. Women always complain that men don't talk, but I think what we really mean is they don't talk about what we want them to talk about. A professor's wife first opened my eyes to the importance of listening to a man by making a terrifying statement. She said, "When we don't actively listen to our husbands we *teach them not to talk to us.*" *Yikes*! I cannot tell you how many times my husband has started to jabber about something as interesting as snail slime, and suddenly, just as I'm starting to tune out, I hear my professor's words in my mind. I snap to attention and engage.

"So why does the carburetor do that? What's so great about that commentary? Who's the best player on the team?" Sometimes it gets interesting, and sometimes it stays as boring as snail slime. But you know what? I'll learn everything there is to know about football if it means he'll talk to me when he's hurting.

Listening is a segue to the heart. In those moments when I'm silencing *Downton Abbey* to listen to all the features of the new Honda Odyssey, he and I are forging a trust. We're building intimacy that says, "I care about you. I care to know what you're thinking about. I care to have a relationship with you." Listening is also the first step toward romancing him because it causes you to think the way he thinks. Maybe he talks a lot about a particular band, so this Valentine's Day, instead of surprising him with a special meal, you surprise him with tickets to a concert. Or maybe he mentions that he's always ready to crash in the afternoon at the office, so you show up at 2pm with Starbucks and a note. Now you're speaking his language, and *that's* romance. (P.S. In order for him to talk, occasionally *you* will need to stop talking. This was a revolutionary insight for me.)

Meet his needs generously.

There's really not a whole lot a guy needs. Honestly. This is one of those surprising things I'm learning from my husband. Female relationships are so complex because the majority of our needs are internal. We don't just want flowers, we want him to connect with us emotionally. However, I think most men see outward action *as* inward connection. Listen to the way they brag—it's almost always action-based. Take my brother-in-law, for instance. He's a woefully sleep-deprived pediatric neurosurgery resident. You know what he brags about? The way the whole house could be a wreck, but his wife will have a clean bed with fresh sheets just for him after he's worked 36 hours straight. I once heard a famous pastor brag about the way his wife fixes his favorite breakfast every Sunday morning. Basic needs, lavishly met. I think it ministers to men more than we realize. At least, I'd wager it's more romantic than keeping him up all night so we can talk about our feelings.

We've talked about two basic needs: sleep and food. Perhaps you're thinking of one other need I've failed to mention. Let me just say, *yes,* I believe it matters too. Honestly, it probably matters more than any of the others! Don't just meet his needs, meet them *generously. Freely. Joyfully*. Meet his needs, knowing that you are actually pursuing his heart.

Respect him.

Because of Ephesians 5 and numerous Christian books, I knew one thing loud and clear before marrying Clint: he craves my respect. What's more, respecting my husband is a biblical mandate. Okay, but what on earth am I supposed to *do*? That's what I always wanted to ask. As a young bride, I didn't really get how to "accomplish" this mandate. Do I just say nice things to him? Tell him I think he's manly? I often wished there was a secret manual of "ten easy ways to make your husband feel respected," so I could check them off.

I look back at that young bride and smile at her naiveté. Because now I get it. The funny thing about respect is it's more easily identified in its absence than its presence. In other words, *disrespecting* my husband is what finally taught me the nature of respect. It's not an action; it's a heart attitude. That young bride, lying awake at night, wondering how she could demonstrate respect for Clint, already respected him in her heart. But the longer we were married, the more I saw his flaws, and the more my heart waned in respect. Which brings me to the greatest lesson I have ever learned regarding respect: *Like faith, respect is proven truest through fire.*

I once asked Clint what I could get for his birthday that would really show him I loved him. He told me, "Honestly, what would really make me feel loved, is if you showed me grace when I fail." I think I bought him a paintball gun. But his words have haunted me ever since. They will often come rushing to mind in the midst of a fight, when I'm so angry I'm ready to go for the jugular, to say something devastatingly disrespectful. In that moment, I think: *this is when it counts, Jeanne!* All the birthday presents in the world can't speak as powerfully as that moment when I'm most angry and I choose to respect him anyway. Remember—that moment, when you *least* want to give it, is your *greatest* opportunity to demonstrate respect.

If you're like me, as you think through romancing the man in your life, you may feel equally inspired and discouraged. The truth is it's *hard* to listen, serve, and respect. Not one of these attributes is sold on the Valentine's Day aisle at Target. And yet...that's *exactly* why each one is infinitely valuable.

The Marriage Conversation You Ought to Have

Here is a true confession: whenever I think about "working on my marriage" I think of Clint's shortcomings before I think of my own. I picture myself sitting down beside him (perhaps with a neatly organized list) and talking through all my complaints, beginning with the petty irritations and working my way to the really irritating irritations. Surely if we could iron those out, we'd be on the fast track to eternal bliss.

Do you want to know how the best marriage conversation I've ever had with Clint started? Completely opposite. I had been reading about confession in a marriage book when I came across this statement: *"It is a sign of God's grace when our consciences are sensitive and our hearts are grieved, not at what the other person is doing, but at what we have become."*[2]

"What we have become"—it felt like a slap in the face because the minute I read it, I knew that I was not proud of what I had become in my marriage. But it had been such a long time since I looked deeply and honestly into my own heart. After all, it was much easier to shine the flashlight on Clint than on myself. But that day, sitting on the sofa, the veil came off.

I asked Clint to come sit beside me, and I confessed. I'm not talking about those little "I ate the last brownie" confessions. I mean I *really* confessed. I confessed my secret fighting strategies for making myself look better than him. I confessed the awful habits that had made me become a wife I never wanted to become. I confessed the sins I normally excused away, on the grounds of "cutting myself a little slack." I confessed as honestly as I could, until I could think of nothing left to confess. As I confessed, I cried. And as I cried, he held me.

You know how as women we always want men to connect with us? We want that moment when he's totally engaged, when all his emotions are tuned in and he just *gets* us. Here's the thing, I always thought I could force that sort of connection by getting him to recognize *his* shortcomings. Not by confessing mine. But that day on the sofa was the most connected I had felt to Clint in a long time. He didn't hug me like he was heading out the door late for work. He hugged me like he loved me with all his heart. And guess what else? *He* began to confess. That day we tasted grace, and it tasted just like the gospel—humble, forgiving, and celebratory.

One thing that surprised me at the end of our discussion was how strangely vulnerable I felt. I think sometimes people who've been married for a while assume that the vulnerability fades between them because they've grown so close. After all, there are no secrets, nothing off-limits...no more vulnerability, right? But actually, the vulnerability might have faded not because they're so close but because they've allowed themselves to grow so distant. The surest way to kill the vulnerability in a marriage is to build up defenses and reinforce them regularly. Choose to win instead of love. Choose to take instead of give. Choose to blame instead of confess. And one day you will realize you don't feel the least bit vulnerable with the man beside you. It won't be because you're close. It'll be because you're hard as a rock.

That's the scary thing about marriage. It can drift apart quietly without you even noticing. It's not like a teenager you can send off to college with a credit card. It's like a newborn baby you have to nurture every single day. In other words, leave it to itself and it will *die.* That's what nobody ever told me about marriage.

But invest in it, sacrifice for it, regularly choose it over yourself, and just like a newborn baby, it can become the delight of your life. Even on the poopy days. Even when the battles are hard won. It's never perfect, but it *can* be a steady foundation, a safe refuge, a joyful allegiance.

Today as I type on my computer, I have no idea what state your marriage is in. But I do know this—I gave you a vulnerable glimpse into mine because I believe marriage is worth fighting for. I wouldn't understand how marriages drift if I didn't have firsthand experience. I couldn't write about pride unless I know exactly how it tastes. So if you (like me) have ever tallied up your spouse's shortcomings, or been reluctant to shine the light on yourself, maybe it's time for a conversation on the sofa. I cannot guarantee the way your spouse will respond, but this I can guarantee: Christ will go with you, empower you, and reward your faithfulness. His shed blood is the reason you and I can humbly confess and wholeheartedly forgive.

Do You Ever Worry You'll Fall Out of Love?

An unmarried friend asked me this question recently, and for one small moment I felt like Mickey Mantle teaching a newbie how to swing. Eight years ago a question like this would've been a fast pitch straight to my head. But not anymore. I smiled and watched the softball lob through the air. As a dreamy romantic who's learned a lot of lessons the hard way, this was one question I knew I could knock out of the park.

Do I ever worry I'll fall out of love? No. Because I already have. If we define love in the ooey-gooey sense, then I've already fallen in and out and back in and back out of love (with the same man!) thousands of times. That night I assured my friend that she could stop worrying about falling out of love not because it's a rarity, but because it's a certainty. It doesn't matter who you marry, at some point the butterflies will fly away and forget to put the toilet seat down when they go. But this is not a bad thing! When those butterflies desert you, they will take with them the fairytale of love, and leave the reality of love in its place.

I know this sounds cringe-worthy, believe me, the Anne of Green Gables within me also wants to cringe. The fairytale of love is everything beautiful about love, right? It's delight instead of duty, passion instead of obligation. But here's the catch. Fairytale love *is* true love... just not for *him.* The reason fairytale love feels so great is because at its core it's love for *me.*

At this point in the conversation I launched into Paul David Tripp's explanation of the two kingdoms in life.[3] (My friend rolled her eyes too, but pay attention! This is the heart of it all.) There are two kingdoms in life: the Kingdom of God and the Kingdom of Self. "Falling in love" naturally caters to the Kingdom of Self. It makes you feel beautiful, special, and skinnier than you actually are. Then you fast forward a decade and realize the Kingdom of Self has taken a major hit. He no longer exists solely to woo you and make you feel good about yourself. Worse yet, he's prone to take an interest in *his* Kingdom of Self...which co-exists with *your* Kingdom of Self about as well as a kingdom can function with two kings and zero servants. At this point, you have a choice. You can continue living for the Kingdom of Self, which will involve slowly shutting him out, filling your life with personal hobbies and distractions, and perhaps finding someone new to "fall in love" with.

Or you can choose to live for the Kingdom of God. The tough part is, the Kingdom of God is radically opposed to **gulp** self. It stays up late to listen when it's aching to go to bed. It wakes up early with the needs and desires of the other fresh on its heart. It forgives painful sins, gets involved in messy problems, and does laundry that's been sitting in the car long enough to make you gag. The Kingdom of God honors others when no one's watching, thinks of others when it doesn't want to, and gives when nobody returns the favor. And when the Kingdom of Self is clawing at your chest, the Kingdom of God tells it to hush, and keeps on serving.

Do you feel hopeless yet? That's a *good* thing because the bottom line is you and I can't ever love this way on our own. That's why we need a Savior. That's why marriage is such a picture of the gospel. Without the grace of Jesus, two sinners could never love the way Christ loves. And here's the really amazing part: this kind of self-denying, other-focused love that is *agonizing* to practice and only possible by God's grace and strength, generates the truest and purest affection you could ever imagine.

Picture a day at the fair, riding on the Ferris Wheel with that handsome boy who's totally consumed with you. Ah, butterflies galore! Now picture that same boy ten years later, crying when he feels like a failure. Vomiting when he's caught a stomach bug. Angry when he has a bad day. Picture looking at him and being able to see his insecurities, his weaknesses, his longings, and his hopes. Picture yourself comforting him when he cries, cleaning up his vomit, forgiving his misplaced anger. None of these actions are devoid of emotion. Neither are they governed by emotion. Rather, they *inspire* emotion. Empathy, devotion, gratitude, contentment, joy, and yes, even passion long after the last butterfly has left.

Two Different Dances

You were a different
Dance than me,
When I smiled
And took your hand.
Closed my eyes
And opened my heart
To the wonders
And mysteries of man.
The dance has been long,
It's only begun,
It's been agonizing,
Jubilant fun.
It's been a muddy haze,
Crystal clear,
Distant and far,
Desperately near.
Two different dances,
Twirling in time,
One lovely waltz,
Sweetly divine.
So, take my hands, darling,
Turn me again,

Promise me always,
Has yet to begin.
For this I know surely,
Wholly and true:
I could dance forever,
If only with you.

Mom

"THE CLOCKS WERE STRIKING MIDNIGHT AND THE ROOMS WERE VERY STILL AS A FIGURE GLIDED QUIETLY FROM BED TO BED, SMOOTHING A COVERLID HERE, SETTLING A PILLOW THERE, AND PAUSING TO LOOK LONG AND TENDERLY AT EACH UNCONSCIOUS FACE, TO KISS EACH WITH LIPS THAT MUTELY BLESSED, AND TO PRAY THE FERVENT PRAYERS WHICH ONLY MOTHERS UTTER."

Louisa May Alcott, *Little Women*

The Rollercoaster

I got on a rollercoaster today.
It didn't seem I had a lot of say,
For I never ran to it in haste,
Yet suddenly I was strapping a seatbelt 'round my waist.

Then up, and up, and up it climbed;
My heart was soaring and so my mind!
At the very top a wedding march played,
Church doors swung open and the bride was displayed!

Just as I thought I'd burst with delight,
My jubilant heart erupted in fright.
Down and down and down we plunged,
'Til we could've soaked up our tears with a 10-gallon sponge.

Whizzing past failure, swooping beneath bills,
I lost all sight of my original will.
My heart was consumed with anxiety and doubt,
What did we think marriage was all about?

Then just as suddenly we began our ascent,
Gathered extra money, even paid our rent!
Accepted into Grad School, a new job for the wife,
Yes, yes! Now this is living the life!

Laughing with friends, hosting parties all night,
Once more I could feel my heart racing with delight.
Security! Stability! Oh, to be young and free!
Wait...wait...wait...what's happening to me?!

Stomach growing rounder, ankles swelling fast,
Plunging lower and lower—the freedom's not gonna last!!
My tummy's churning madly; I'm puking left and right,
Now suddenly I'm in a rocking chair, crying through the night.

Eyes so bleary, mind so crazy, body worn and stretchy,
The rollercoaster's reached its low...and boy does it look messy.
Poopy diapers, spit-up rags, mommy always crying,
Whoever said it'd be sheer bliss surely must've been lying.

And then one day a little coo,
A giggle, a smile, a babble—who knew?
A night full of sleep and those first sweet words,
Motherhood, difficult? Don't be absurd!

She's darling, she's perfect, she's utterly sweet!
Look! Look! She took a step on her two little feet!
Laughing all day, giving Mommy a kiss,
Life doesn't get any better than this!

The coaster's soaring high, the wind in my hair,
She is the greatest answer to prayer!
She's mine forever and I'll never leave her,
Wait just a minute...is that a FEVER??

Down, down we go flying in the blink of an eye;
What if it's incurable...what if she dies??
What if she's rebellious and my world falls apart?
What if some loser breaks her heart?

How much more can I take? This coaster's a bear!
I look left and right—are we getting anywhere?
And then I glance backwards and suddenly I know,
I've been on this ride forever and there's forever left to go.

I stare at the track swerving up ahead:
Jobs, babies, trials...I'll be riding 'til I'm dead!
"Stop the rollercoaster!" I scream into the air.
It screeches to a halt and I scurry from my chair.

"What is this hellish ride?" I demand to know out loud,
Glaring at the driver through eyes like darkened clouds.
"This ride is filled with turmoil; it's insanity and strife!"
He calmly looks at me and says, "The ride is called 'Life.' "

"I hate it!" I yell. "I can't do it, I know!"
He pauses to consider, then answers kind of slow.
"Perhaps this isn't the ride for you;
I'll tell you what you ought to do.

Head to the line you see on that hill,
The passengers say that ride is still.
It's calm and it's steady; some even claim
They can sense joy on the parts filled with pain."

"Yes, yes!" I nod quickly. "That's the ride for me!
Oh, thank you and good-bye!" I shout out with glee.
I pause and turn back, one thing left to say,
"Just tell me what it's called, so I don't lose my way!"

Already my heart is light; the peace I nearly taste
As he looks at me and says, "They call that ride 'Faith.' "

How a Baby Changes Your Life

The first time I was pregnant I made one big mistake. Amid taking vitamins, swimming laps in the seminary pool, and reading pregnancy books, I learned absolutely nothing about what to do when the baby actually arrived. It's like I never realized that the pretty glow and stretchy clothes weren't the final destination. I was the happiest, (largest), most naïve pregnant lady alive.

And then she came.

Good-bye happy glowing pregnant lady. Hello zombie-mommy—as terrified, exhausted, and clueless as the wiggling infant in my arms. I was overwhelmed by a desperate, protective love for this little person, yet I'd never felt more incompetent in my whole life. It's like I had the most important job in the universe with the intelligence of a third grader. I shoved my stash of pregnancy books into the closet, and became a voracious reader of baby-raising manuals. Unfortunately, reading in the middle of the night while nursing and simultaneously sobbing into a burp cloth is not exactly the opportune time for learning how to raise a baby. To make matters worse, I quickly discovered that no two baby-raising "experts" on the face of the planet have ever agreed about a single thing.

In His great kindness, God walked with me, taught me, and sustained me. I came to learn that there are stages in adjusting to parenthood. If you're pregnant and well-prepared, feel free to skip right along to the next chapter. But if you're a full-bellied, blissfully ignorant beauty, keep reading! This one's for you. It's everything I wish someone had told me before embarking on the journey.

Stage 1: The Twilight Zone

The initial weeks following baby's birth can feel a bit like entry into a parallel universe. There were two changes in particular that threw me the most. For starters, if your baby is biological, it's possible to feel like a stranger in your own body. Simultaneously, you experience physical recovery from the delivery, a surge of new hormones, lactation, and a postpartum figure you may find disappointing. Secondly, baby is born with zero regard for your current schedule. Her life is a continuous cycle of eating and sleeping, which means you enter an eerie new world where you don't think in terms of night and day. You think in terms of 2-3 hour cycles that include feeding, burping, crying and sleeping over and over again all through the day *and night.* (Do you remember that scene in *Men in Black* when Tommy Lee Jones tells Will Smith that they work on Centaurian time and he'll either get used to it or have a psychotic breakdown? It's a little like that.)

So how do you prepare for this? Make a deal with yourself now that during the Twilight Zone Stage, you are excused from guilt—no need to fit into your skinny jeans, clean the whole house, or smile all the time. Feeling sad or overwhelmed doesn't mean you're a bad mom; it means you're *human*, and you're adjusting. Just giving yourself this sort of grace can free you immensely to enjoy your little one without all the pressure. Secondly, ENLIST HELP! The Twilight Zone Stage is no time to be a hero. Accept every casserole that comes your way, even if it means you have to answer the door in your pajamas. It will be worth it. Especially if they packed dessert. Invite your mom, or mother-in-law to move in for a few weeks. It doesn't matter if she gets on your nerves a little; if she's willing to clean a toilet, cook dinner, and hold the baby at 2am, she'll be worth her weight in gold! Finally, begin to pray now for patience, perspective, and gratitude. For all its challenges, the Twilight Zone Stage can be one of the most precious seasons of your life—a season in which God sanctifies you, amazes you with His grace, and blesses you more richly than you could ever imagine.

Stage 2: The Philosophy Crisis

Once the initial blur of "newness" begins to wear off, you will find yourself contemplating numerous daily decisions. Do you want to put baby on a schedule? How soon will you implement the schedule? Will you let baby cry? What will you do if baby won't sleep? Do you want to co-sleep? Do you want to train baby to sleep independently?

In short, there are two major approaches when it comes to raising an infant. There is the "parent-directed" philosophy which relies heavily on establishing a schedule, and the "attachment" philosophy which advocates following baby's cues and natural instincts for closeness. Here's the tricky thing: these two approaches are not isolated options. They are opposite ends of a *spectrum* of options. Most people don't fall entirely into one camp, but land somewhere between the two, which is why it feels like experts never agree with each other. For instance, I couldn't peg James Dobson as a "scheduling" advocate or an "attachment" advocate because he accepts and rejects different components of *both* approaches. And it's likely you will, too, the more you grow with your baby.

So how do you prepare? Think of two or three moms who meet the following criteria: you admire them as a woman and mother, they have *young* children, and their personality is similar to yours.

This is your best bet for an "advice-giver." Ask these moms for their very best "new baby" advice, and don't just put them on the spot. Let them think about it and get back to you later. This way you'll really get their best thoughts. Ask them which books were the most helpful and read them. Talk to your husband about what you're learning and get his feedback. Finally, resolve to hold your newfound opinions *tentatively.* Becoming dogmatic (especially before little Lucy even arrives) can make you highly critical of yourself and of others.

Stage 3: The Grace-Filled Rhythm

With each of my daughters, between 4-6 months, it felt as though normalcy returned. Of course every day still held a degree of unpredictability, but by and large, life fell back into a steady rhythm. I knew what to expect and how to respond. It may happen sooner for you, or take a little longer, but know this—as surely as The Twilight Zone is coming, normalcy will make a return.

You've seen me reading my baby books and sobbing in my rocking chair. Now fast forward five years. Do you see the preschooler drawing a picture at the kitchen table? The toddler dancing in her underwear? The Daddy monster bursting through the door every afternoon to tickle all the bellybuttons in sight? I do. I live in a world where a can of glitter can make you a hero for the day, and two little braids dancing in the wind is enough to make you wish time would stand still forever. My point is, when they tell you "this too shall pass," no matter how much you want to slap them, it really is true. *Virtually every challenge you face with a baby will eventually pass.* This is not true for older children. There's no guarantee that every child will submit to Christ, marry a godly spouse, or live out his full potential. But *every* child will eventually sleep through the night. As my doctor likes to remind me, nobody breastfeeds in elementary school or takes a pacifier to college. The trials are momentary. The rewards are eternal.

Freedom from Fearful Parenting

Fear was the first thing that ever drove me to God. It wasn't fear *of* God, it was fear of everything else. As a small child I lived in constant fear that my parents would die. By the time I was eleven-years-old I had developed an enslaving fear of demons that I would battle for nearly four years. I remember telling my mom I didn't believe I would ever break free. *But I did.* One painstaking day at a time, my parents taught me to quote truth in the face of fear over and over again, sometimes thirty times a day. And then twenty. And then ten, as the bouts grew smaller and my faith grew bigger. Until one day I realized I couldn't remember the last time a fear of demons had controlled me.

That journey radically influenced my perspective of fear. It took the "fear" out of fear because it taught me that fear is conquerable. It taught me that fear is really all about deception. It's about fooling us into forgetting the character and reality of God. I love the way our children's Bible captures the account of Jesus calming the storm. *"'Why were you scared?' Jesus asked. 'Did you forget who I Am? Did you believe your fears, instead of me?'"*[4]

Even as I type the words, my heart whispers *yes.* Yes, Jesus, even as an adult I forget who You are. I am tempted, continually, to believe my fears instead of You. Recently, a new mom contacted me to suggest I write about fear, specifically in parenting. This is a portion of what she wrote:

> Since becoming a mom, one thing that I didn't expect was the fear that has accompanied my new role. Fear that I'm not doing a good job, fear that I'll hurt him, fear that I hear him crying while he's napping and I'm in the shower, fear he will wake up in the middle of the night screaming, fear that he's not eating right, fear that he'll have allergies...the list goes on and on.

Can you relate? I sure can. Parenting has this unique way of opening up worlds of fear we didn't even contemplate pre-children. And unfortunately (as wiser moms have taught me) the temptation to fear doesn't bid you farewell when your kids get older. It only grows and expands like spaghetti in a pot. Either get a handle on it or call Strega Nona!

So how do we get a handle on it? The same way I did seventeen years ago. By claiming truth in the face of fear, moment by scary moment. *(See the chart I've compiled of common fears and biblical truths.)*

As we intentionally train our children in godliness, we must also actively trust that the days and experiences allotted for them are in the hands of God.[5] Only then will we experience peace in parenting.

Years ago, my mother spoke a Bible verse over my life: "It is the Lord of hosts whom you should regard as holy. And He shall be your fear, and He shall be your dread. Then He shall become a sanctuary."[6] I didn't understand it at the time, but it's beautiful to me now. The secret to freedom from fear is *fear of God.* If you and I tremble at the power, dominion, and Lordship of God Almighty, we will tremble at nothing else. We will remember that the Captain of the Storm is still in the boat. And *He* will be our sanctuary.

	Common Fears	Trustworthy Truths
Physical	Life-threatening sickness or injury will befall my child.	"All the days ordained for (my child) were written in Your book before one of them came to be." Ps 139:16
	My child will fall into the hands of evil people (kidnapping, abuse...etc.)	"Do not be afraid of those who kill the body but cannot kill the soul...Are not two sparrows sold for a penny? Yet not one of them will fall to the ground apart from the will of your Father. And even the very hairs of (my child's) head are numbered. So don't be afraid; (your child) is worth more than many sparrows." Mt 10:28-31
	Something will be "wrong" with my child developmentally.	"For You created (my child's) inmost being; you knit (him/her) together in (my) womb. I praise you because (my child) is fearfully and wonderfully made; Your works are wonderful, I know that full well." Ps 139:13-14
	My child will experience unique suffering because of a disability.	"But he said to me, 'My grace is sufficient for you, for my power is made perfect in weakness.' Therefore (my child can) boast all the more gladly about (his/her) weaknesses, so that Christ's power may rest on (him/her)...For when (my child) is weak, then (my child) is strong." 2 Cor 12:9-10
Emotional and/or Social	My child will be rejected by peers.	"Am I now trying to win the approval of men, or of God? Or am I trying to please men? If I were still trying to please men, I would not be a servant of Christ." Gal 1:10
	My child will experience failure that damages his/her self-esteem.	"And we know that in all things God works for the good of those who love Him, who have been called according to His purpose." Rom 8:28
	A trauma we're going through in our family will adversely affect my child's well-being.	"I know whom I have believed, and am convinced that He is able to guard what I have entrusted to Him..." 2 Tm 1:12
Spiritual	My child will reject God.	"No one can come to Me unless the Father who sent Me draws him." Jn. 6:44 "(The Lord) is patient with you, not wanting anyone to perish, but everyone to come to repentance." 2 Pt 3:9
	Ungodly peers will influence my child.	"...He who began a good work in (my child) will carry it on to completion until the day of Christ Jesus." Phil 1:6
	I am an inadequate spiritual leader; I will "mess my child up."	"For it is by grace you have been saved, through faith--and this not from yourselves, it is the gift of God--not by works, so that no one can boast." Eph 2:8-9
	Sinful strongholds in my life will be passed on to my child.	"Therefore if anyone is in Christ, he is a new creation; the old has gone, the new has come!" 2 Cor 5:17

What Kids Really Want

America has long been hailed as the land of opportunities. Every decade they seem to grow exponentially. Do you want to start your own business? Self-publish a book? Become a YouTube rock star? It's never been easier. But we aren't the only ones with ever-widening opportunities. Our kids are growing up in a world few of their grandparents could've imagined. No longer is summer about trading baseball cards and kicking around a soccer ball. It's about science camp, ballet lessons, downloading Apps, online gaming, and gluten-free, dairy-free, GMO-free snacks in BPA-free containers. *Options.* If there's one thing we have as parents in the 21st century, it's options. Which is a good thing, right?

A few months ago we went to a restaurant in Kentucky that served only grilled cheese sandwiches. How they took America's simplest sandwich and came up with 58 options on their menu is beyond me. But I'll say this, I felt like my brain cells were shrinking as I spent twenty minutes trying to pick a grilled cheese sandwich. Yes, options provide opportunities, but they also complicate life. As parents, they create an undercurrent of pressure. We want (and often feel compelled) to give our kids everything. Every advantage, every opportunity, every collectible My Little Pony Equestrian doll. We want to nurture every talent, support every interest, and cater to every preference. Because after all, isn't that what the Joneses are doing?

This summer I agonized to the point of insanity over school options for my eldest. Did I mention she is entering pre-K? As in *pre*-Kindergarten. As in the grade *before* the grade in which you spend 30% of the day coloring. But you know what? I love my daughters. This is why I agonize. But it's not the only reason I agonize. I also agonize because I don't trust God. And because I idolize my children's well-being. And because I'm arrogant enough to want to be the best mom in the world.

Last month my husband suggested we read a little book by Kevin DeYoung called *Crazy Busy. (Hmm…I wonder why he thought we needed to read that?)* Among other things, the book presents seven diagnoses to consider regarding our crazy busy lives. I was especially struck by diagnosis #4: "You Need to Stop Freaking Out about Your Kids." (Kevin's words, not mine!) He cites a survey conducted by Ellen Galinsky in which more than a thousand school-aged children were asked what one thing they would change about how their parents' work affected them. Parents were surprised to find that the children seldom wished for more time with them. Rather, the vast majority wished their parents were less tired and less stressed. DeYoung borrows the term "secondhand stress" to describe the way children feel in a constantly frazzled environment. Listen to this:

> By trying to do so much for them, we are actually making our kids less happy. It would be better for us and for our kids if we planned fewer outings, got involved in fewer activities, took more breaks from the kids, did whatever we could to get more help around the house, and made parental sanity a higher priority.[7]

The first time I read this, I had to re-read it. *Wait a minute—did he just say take* ***more*** *breaks from the kids? Get* ***more*** *help around the house?*

*By doing these things, I may end up being a **better** parent for them?* I found myself exhaling. In the tightrope of parenting, it felt like someone had just cut me some much needed slack. If DeYoung is right, and what my kids really want (although they are too young to express it) is a mom who is at peace, then maybe I don't need to feel so guilty every time I drop my girls off with a babysitter. Or say "No" to soccer camp three states away. Or throw a pizza in the oven and pop in a movie. Maybe these aren't the "survival" choices, but occasionally, the better ones. The ones that de-frazzle the week, lower the hyper-high-performance bar, and give my kids the sense of calm they ache for.

Maybe all this goes to show that parenting ought to be less about *doing* and more about *being*. Less about co-sleeping debates and pacifier anxiety, and more about becoming a woman centered on Christ. Less about performancc and guilt, and more about *daily* finding hope in the grace of the gospel. Because despite the fact that my kids still beg for the things everyone else has, one day when they look back on their childhood, they'll remember more than all the activities and opportunities. They'll remember what *kind* of home they had, be it peaceful…or crazy busy.

3 Ways to Raise a Pharisee

If anyone could do a fantastic job raising a Pharisee, it's me. I have always identified more with the elder brother than the prodigal son, a dangerous association indeed.[8] Recently a mom wrote to me asking for advice about helping her two-year-old daughter recognize her need for Jesus. I was so touched by this mom's passionate desire to point her young daughter to Christ as the only hope for righteousness. It is the exact opposite of Pharisaism, which looks to oneself for righteousness. The question got me thinking about the three biggest mistakes I've made as a parent that point my children toward works-based performance:

Get more excited about what they do, then who they're becoming.

"Mommy look, I drew a stick." "OH MY GOODNESS, IT'S FABULOUS!!" That's me. A year ago, a statement in C.J. Mahaney's book *Humility* changed my perspective. He wrote that he reserves his highest praise for examples of true greatness—sacrifice, humility, love, service—the things *Jesus* has deemed great.[9] I realized I did cartwheels over my kids' artwork and I said, "that's kind" when they shared their toys. I still show delight in their artwork and dance moves and all the other skills they love to show me, but I try to reserve greater excitement for evidence of Christ at work in their lives. Because at the end of the day it's not about what they can do. It's about what Christ has done, and continues to do, for them.

Give them credit for acts of righteousness.

Around the time my firstborn turned two, I began exclaiming, "Good girl!" whenever she obeyed. Since obedience from a two-year-old is a rare commodity indeed, the words were like honey on my tongue, "Good girl! You obeyed Mommy!" One day she walked through the house thumping her chest and proudly declaring, "I a good girl!" And just like that it hit me. *No. Actually you're not.* My little girls are many things—precious, beautiful, sensitive, smart—but they are not inherently *good.* The Bible teaches that there is *none* righteous, that *all* have sinned and fallen short of God's glory.[10] The last thing I want to do is make my daughters foolishly believe that they don't need God, when in reality, apart from Christ, all their good works are filthy rags before Him. I started saying, "Wise choice! Jesus helped you obey Mommy! He helped you make a wise choice! Isn't He great?" Two years later, that same sweet child has caught me giving her praise and said, "Jesus helped me do it, Mommy." I've never been so blessed to be corrected.

Compare them to others.

As an education major in college I was taught that a "positive" method of correcting wrong behavior is to praise right behavior. So when you notice Steven acting like a hooligan, you loudly say, "I like the way *Johnny* is sitting quietly." At best it's manipulative, at worst it's Pharisaism in training. But it's so tempting because it's effective. Johnny's chest puffs up, Steven's shoulders sag, and the hooligan is back in line. At home it looks like this: "Look at your big brother. Is *he* swinging from the chandelier?" Before long, every time you correct the little brother, the big brother will point out his obedience for you. "*I* am not interrupting. *I* am sitting still. *I* am listening." You want to raise a Pharisee? This is one of the fastest ways. And I confess I'm guilty as charged.

Lest you're tempted to hang your head in discouragement right about now, remember: as you point your kids to the grace of Christ, don't forget to drink deeply of it yourself. Johnny and Steven aren't the only people who gravitate toward legalism. And as we raise them, we must trust that Christ is sovereign over our parenting. After all, if He could use eleven weak and broken disciples to build His world-wide church, He can use one weak and broken Mama to demonstrate the glory of His gospel to the children He has entrusted to her.

Assessing the Princess Obsession

One day, about a month before her third birthday, I casually asked Aubrey what sort of party she'd like. She stared at me blankly. Because I'm not a do-it-yourself kind of gal, I thought of the limited party-plate selection at Walmart, and prompted, "You know, like a Dora party or a princess party?" Aubrey considered for a moment, then announced, "I want a princess party." Okay, done! Immediately I thought of the $5 Ariel costume I'd picked up at a consignment sale for trick-or-treating. Perfect! There were 86 billion princess party supplies at Walmart, and she could wear her Ariel costume twice.

But in the weeks that followed, I began to have second-thoughts. As Heidi's first birthday came and went, Aubrey grew increasingly excited about her upcoming princess party. She talked about princesses, watched movies about princesses, and adoringly dressed the Polly Pocket princesses at her friend's house. My doubts grew. But I'd already told Grandma about the princess party, and the day after she heard, all 86 billion princess party supplies from Walmart were deposited on my dining room table, along with a stash of princess coloring books to last through the Apocalypse. Before long, Aubrey knew all the Disney princesses by name and dress color. Images of *Toddlers in Tiaras* began to dance through my mind unbidden. Finally, one night, I voiced my concerns to Clint.

"You know, I've been thinking…what if we did a 'God's princess' theme? We could put up a big sign that says, 'I know I'm a princess because my Father is the King of Kings!'"

"Sounds kinda cheesy," Clint said.

**Sigh.* Back to the drawing board. In the end, I kept the princess theme. Aubrey wore little orange hair extensions with her Ariel costume (absolutely adorable), and I made a grossly disproportional under-the-sea cake complete with Barbie Ariel stuck on top. When the last princess plate was thrown away and the kids were tucked in bed, I finally sat down and asked myself why the whole fiasco concerned me so much.

I realized it's because there's something beautiful and dangerous in the princess theme. I never taught my girls to be enraptured by princesses. I doubt many moms do. And yet, the phenomenon lives. Why? Because it captures the female heart. It speaks of our desire to be precious, treasured, and loved. All of these messages I want to drive deeply into my daughters' hearts: *you are precious, lovely, and valuable because God Almighty created You, gave His life to redeem you, and pursues you even now. You will never meet a King as mighty, nor a Prince as romantic as Jesus Himself. In belonging to Him you will find all the worth your soul ever craves.*

But this is only one side of the coin. The princess theme is also engaging because it caters to our sinful longing to make much of ourselves. And that is the aspect of the princess obsession that makes me cringe. Not the desire to be special, but the desire to be the *most* special, the most beautiful, the most important, the most *glorified.* As a mother who desperately loves my daughters, I see a powerful beast alive in the princess mentality, and it makes me want to don some knightly armor and rescue my girls myself. I want to protect them from the arrogance of entitlement, the addiction to self-glory as ancient as the Tower of Babel. But the truth is, plastering a cheesy banner across my living room wall doesn't make me a knight any more than fastening orange extensions into Aubrey's hair makes her Ariel. There is only One Warrior with the ability to protect my daughters, only One Hero with the capacity to satisfy them. And my greatest hope for raising my girls in godliness is daily throwing myself upon His mercy.

5 Reasons I Fear Standing Up to My Kids

I PREFER TO CHOOSE WHAT'S EASY OVER WHAT'S BEST.

There is a mentality with the little years that says, *just get through it!* In other words, the goal is survival. And believe me, *I get it.* What's more, on many occasions, I live by it. It's shortcut parenting, and it comes so naturally. Toss the insomniac newborn in a swing for six months. Bribe the stubborn toddler. Negotiate with the manipulative preschooler. But what I didn't realize is adopting the shortcut mentality is like financing a mansion with no money down. Free today, and a nightmare when the cost catches up with you. When the insomniac baby outgrows the swing. When the easily bribed toddler becomes the out-of-control third grader. When the manipulative preschooler morphs into the argumentative teenager who could outtalk the District Attorney.

In contrast, the mandate of Proverbs 22:6 to train our children in the discipline and instruction of the Lord, carries an opposite promise: "even when they are old they will not turn from it."

I LOVE MYSELF MORE THAN I LOVE THEM.

One morning I picked up one of my kids after Bible study only to have her erupt in a fit of tears when I told her to put on her coat. As the hallway began to fill and people began to stare, her teacher burst into spontaneous song: "O is for Obey! O is for Obey! Obey means doing what you should, O is for Obey!" I imagined the cyanide tablets they give soldiers in extreme circumstances, and wished I had one to pop in my mouth.

I quickly muttered, "Fine! Don't wear the coat!" and shoved it into my bag. On the walk to the car, I told myself I was just choosing my battles. But the truth is I was choosing to act in *my* best interest instead of hers. Of course it was in her best interest to wear the coat in the middle of January, but more importantly, it was in her best interest to learn that defiance reaps discipline, and obedience reaps blessing. Proverbs 19:28 says that failing to discipline our children is like *setting our hearts on putting them to death*. It is the opposite of love; in fact the Bible refers to it as a form of hatred: "Whoever spares the rod hates his son, but he who loves him is diligent to discipline him."[11] *Ouch!* How's that for a convicting verse? When I abdicate my authority to save face, I am loving myself more than my children.

I'm swayed by the opinions of the world.

Several months ago, an article on my blog gained widespread criticism. It used the d-word (discipline) and it taught that children are born sinful, two concepts I quickly learned are as popular as telemarketers and sales tax. While some people shared their differing opinions respectfully, there were many who did not. Months later, my heart still races when I think about the influx of hate mail. I was attacked on the two fronts I hold most dear—being a mother and being a Christian. For several weeks as I cried and processed the comments, I didn't discipline my children at all. I was terrified that standing up to them was somehow abusive. In the end, it was my husband who helped root me once more in Scripture, an unchanging foundation in an ever-changing culture.

I'm earthly-minded instead of eternity-minded. In the humdrum of daily living, it's hard to remember that there's more at stake than soggy cereal and wasted toilet paper. But as I read the Word, I'm constantly reminded that the call to follow Christ is not for the faint of heart! It requires denying our flesh, loving Jesus more than anything else, suffering for Him even to the point of death, and enduring until the end. Which means I must prepare my children to be persecuted. I must teach them to live for a greater purpose than pleasure. To do things even when they don't want to do them because they're living for Someone whom the Bible calls us to love supremely. The crazy thing is, all this teaching takes place in the humdrum moments. It's a *lifestyle*, which means our home is a training ground with eternal purposes, for eternal rewards. If the goal is simply to get them in bed on time and off to college someday, then it doesn't really matter whether or not you stand your ground in the details. But if the goal is teaching them to love and submit to the authority of Christ, then it does.

I fail to recognize abdication of authority as sin against God. When I was an education major, a Christian professor told me that our authority as a teacher comes directly from God Himself. Therefore, exercising godly authority is not merely an issue of being effective or maintaining order, it's an issue of *obedience to God*. When I learned this, it changed the conviction with which I embraced my authority. As a parent, it's easy to forget that the calling to be in authority over our children is a divine calling, invented and issued by God.[12] Slowly and uncomfortably, I am learning that to give it up for the sake of convenience, appearance, or my own feelings, is nothing short of sin against my Maker.

There you have it—five reasons I fear standing up to my kids. But there's another way to look at this list. If we flip these statements around, we can also find hidden within, five *motivations* for standing up to our kids. Why do we parent with godly authority? Because it's in the best interest of our children. Because we love them. Because we're governed by the opinions of God, not the world. Because the implications are eternal. And because God Himself has called us to do it. Is it difficult and exhausting? Absolutely. Is it worth it? *Absolutely.*

When Mom Just Needs a Good Cry

Occasionally Clint comes home to the kind of house the biblical womanhood books urge us to cultivate—peaceful, joyful, and in order. Often he comes home to the slightly more frazzled version. But every now and then he comes home to the blank-faced, empty-eyed, wife-of-exhaustion home. Last week I had one of those nights. If I was a punching bag I'd have been entirely flat. All done. He found me sweaty and woefully shower-deprived, chopping sweet potatoes in the kitchen, vacantly wondering if one roasted starch could qualify as dinner. Clint took one look at me and said, "Why don't you go out for dinner tonight? I'll feed the kids and put them to bed."

For a moment I thought the clouds might part and a dove descend from heaven. "Are you *serious*?" Before he could answer (or change his mind) I was in and out of the shower, running out the front door with wet hair and the first pair of clothes I could find.

"Where are you going to eat?" Clint called.

I flashed him a mile-long smile. "I don't care!!"

For an hour and a half I enjoyed sushi, shrimp, and sweet silence. But here is a really honest admission—sometimes, even in the oasis, I feel anxiety. I think it's because deep down I'm afraid I will always end up back here, in this place of depletion and discouragement. And I want to grow past that. After all, I'm an overcomer in Christ. I have three beautiful children who are watching me. And let's be honest, there's not always going to be a Japanese steakhouse when I need it.

So the question I've been asking myself is *what drives me to this point?* When I was a teacher there were stressful days, but I never felt like a coma would be welcome relief. I don't know if it's the ultimate answer, but one of the conclusions I've drawn is that parenthood is just *different* than any other vocational calling. Most jobs allow for a sense of separation. You clock in and clock out. You maintain personal boundaries. You become as emotionally invested (or detached) as you want.

And then along comes children, and in five seconds flat they invade *all* of you, running full speed ahead into your heart, mind, and shower. I used to think that after having kids Clint and I would sometimes still live like we didn't have them. Maybe we'd go on a romantic vacation, or hire a sitter and go out with friends. And we did. But what I didn't realize is that once you have kids, they are *always* a part of you. Even when they're not around physically, you *think* about them, *pray* for them, and wonder if Grandma remembered to put their toe cream on before bed. They are woven into your DNA. It's surreal and precious. It's the reason I cry every time another candle on the birthday cake reminds me that they'll one day be grown.

And at the same time, it's *challenging*. Kids don't ask for a portion of your heart or a little bit of your effort. They ask for all of you. They *need* all of you. When you want to burst into tears because you just had a fight with a friend, they're right there beside you wanting to know, "Why are you crying? What's wrong? Explain it to me, Mom. Help me understand this world, Mom. I'm hungry, Mom. Meet my needs, Mom. Be there *for me,* Mom."

But here's the game changer. You and I have a Parent, too. And unlike us, He's perfect. John 1:12 says, "To all who received Him, to those who believed in His name, He gave the right to become children of God." If you have taken Christ at His Word, surrendering your life to Him because you believe He is who He says He is, then *you are His child.* Which means *you* are allowed to run into His arms and burst into tears just like your baby runs into yours.

And boy, are the arms of Jesus tender. In Matthew 23, even as He is rebuking Jerusalem, Jesus says, "Jerusalem, Jerusalem, you who kill the prophets and stone those sent to you, how often I have longed to gather your children together, as a hen gathers her chicks under her wings, but you were not willing."

O Jesus, I am willing. I am willing to be gathered into your arms. I am willing to find strength in Your strength and rest in Your rest.[13] I am willing—I am *longing*—to be parented by You.

Raising Pure Kids in an Impure World

I still remember the conversation. We were sitting in a coffee shop, three married women with zero kids between us, talking about purity. All of a sudden one of the women exclaimed, "Can you just imagine trying to teach your kids to be pure? Where would you even begin?" Three years later, another mom looked at me and said, "I had sex as a teenager. Honestly, I don't even think it's possible to raise sexually pure kids. If it is, I have no idea how to do it." Both of these women were right about one thing: in and of ourselves we are incapable of raising pure kids. The Bible says God is sovereign, He has ordained all our children's days, and they will be held accountable before Him for their own lives.[14]

But does this mean we shrug and say, "Sounds like a lost cause to me"? As Paul would say, may it never be! We are still called to train, shepherd, and instruct our children. Let me pause and state the obvious here: I don't have teenagers. I don't even have a six-year-old, yet. This is one article I'm not qualified to write as a parent. So let me write it as a child. It wasn't that long ago that *I* was a teenager, wrestling with the issue of sexual purity. By His grace, I believe my parents were the most influential tool God used in helping me stay sexually pure. The following are five principles I've drawn from my experience growing up under godly parents.

Raise your children with a gospel-centered worldview regarding sex and marriage.

I think it's tempting to take a spitball approach when it comes to teaching kids about purity. We present a list of isolated truths about babies, STDs, and future spouses. But they don't need a handful of toppings; they need the whole pizza. Like every other issue, they need us to put it into the context of the gospel, teaching them who they are, who God is, what Christ did on the cross, and how it impacts sex, marriage, and His glory. All this to say...

Give them a greater appreciation for sex.

Say what? Isn't that like giving an Eskimo more snow? The truth is none of us want our sweet children to wind up pregnant with syphilis and a broken heart. So the temptation is to give them a lower view of sex, to emphasize its dangers and dampen the appeal. But what we actually need to do is give them a *higher* view of sex. We need to take their narrow perspective of this feel-good thing and STRETCH it to include the eternal design of a vast God. We need them to be awed by the fact that sex is a sacred gift, invented by God to unite two people in worship of the Creator.

When I was in high school a friend told me she thought open-marriage was no big deal. "You're telling me, you wouldn't mind if your husband had sex with other people?" I asked. I'll never forget her response. She said, "For you sex is this big, special thing. I don't see it that way. For me, it's just sex." It was the first time I realized that Christians are *more* passionate about sex than non-Christians.

Help them see themselves as image-bearers of God.

I once counseled a teenage girl with a laundry list of heartache: cutting, bulimia, bisexuality. You know what she sobbed the most over? Her father. She never believed he loved her. As we talked, the strangest memory came to mind. I was a teenager, working on the computer with my feet on the desk. My dad walked by and said, "Look at those cute toes!" At the time it embarrassed me. *Oh my gosh, Dad, I'm not 3 years old.* But sitting with this girl I realized just how deeply I have always been assured of my father's love. There's never been a moment when I doubted that even my *toes* were precious to him. And without realizing it, I carried this confidence into my relationships with guys. I believed I was made in God's image and worth respecting, because my father—the first man I ever knew—treated me as such.

Assure them of your unconditional love and forgiveness. Of all the times my parents talked with me about purity, the conversation that stands out the most wasn't about staying pure, it was about failing to be pure. My mom said, "I want you to know that if you wind up pregnant, or make every mistake there is, I will always love you and be there for you." Looking back, I realize she chose to motivate me the way Christ does, with a *relationship,* not with fear and the pressure to perform. This brings me to my final point:

Let them know that nothing is off-limits when it comes to talking with you.

Kids quickly learn to test the water before diving in. I still remember an old friend telling me about a conversation he had with his dad in middle school. He asked his father if he'd ever had "weird" dreams... you know, like about *girls*? At the time my friend was probably doing a whole lot more than just dreaming about girls, but he was lobbing a softball question at his dad. His father frowned, barked, *"No!"* and that was the first and last conversation they ever had about purity. Having a voice into the lives of our kids starts with having an ear into their world.

If I employed every one of these principles, would it guarantee that my kids are protected from the pain of impurity? Of course not. All the while we shepherd our children, we realize the results are in God's hands...which is really the best part. If God could turn the greatest persecutor of the church into the greatest missionary for the church, He can use the most sexually active teenager to one day impact the world for Christ. And He can use an imperfect mom with a painful past to begin a legacy of godliness in her family. We serve a God who delights in using foolish, weak, and lowly things for His great glory, so together we may boast in Christ alone.[15]

It's Okay to Admit It's Hard

Sometimes motherhood feels exhilarating. And if we're honest, sometimes it feels like being poked to death by plastic spoons. Like fighting the battle of Thermopylae with a team of Barbie dolls. You want to hear a true confession? This morning when I asked my kids what they want to be when they grow up, my four-year-old blurted, "I want to be a mommy!" And for one millisecond, all I could think was, *"Why??"*

Don't get me wrong; it was flattering. She wants to be me. But the truth is, some days I don't even want to be me! Being me—and I'm sure being you—is hard work. It can be thankless work, lonely and menial. And it can be joyful work, rewarding and energizing. But always, it is *work* in that it requires a reservoir of strength, persistence, and dedication, sometimes with giggles and marshmallow crafts, and sometimes with migraines and diarrhea diapers.

Perhaps the hardest work of motherhood is the work done not with our hands, but our hearts. This work starts at conception, the moment we begin to love the life growing inside of us. It is the work of entrusting back to God what He has entrusted to us. The work of passionate affection and painful surrender. Of giving a faithful God our most fragile treasure. Of lessons slow learned and victories hard won. It is the work of prayer and tears, of snapshot moments sealed in our souls and quiet hopes for the future. One day, it will be the work of letting go. The work of college applications and bridal gowns and empty bedrooms that once wore butterfly quilts. And already I know that on that day, I will long to trade such work for ten thousand diarrhea diapers.

Teddy Roosevelt once said, "Nothing in the world is worth having or worth doing unless it means effort, pain, (and) difficulty." Which makes me think, maybe it's okay to admit motherhood requires gargantuan effort. Maybe it's okay to admit it's painful and difficult. Perhaps motherhood isn't worthwhile *in spite of* the difficulty, but *because* of it. Like a farmer who pours blood, sweat, and tears into his land, we pour *all* of ourselves into our children. And when we think there's nothing left to give, we give a little more. And motherhood becomes beautiful because over the years we have wrestled all the rocks and roots out of that stubborn land, and we have made it *valuable.*

You know what I find amazing? The fact that in spite of her Oscar the Grouchy mom, my four-year-old daughter already recognizes the beauty and value of motherhood. She sees some of the work—the plowing, and planting, and sweating, and crying. But she *focuses* on the fruit. The cradling, and kissing, and singing, and smiling. And when I look at motherhood through her eyes, I find that I'm grateful to be a mom. And especially, to be *her* mom.

The Mom Who Lies

Believe it or not, your chatty toddler is not the most talkative person in your life. You are. To quote the provocative book *Dangerous Calling*:

> No one is more influential in your life than you are, because no one talks to you more than you do. Whether you realize it or not, you are in an unending conversation with yourself, and the things you say to you about you are formative of the way that you live.[16]

I've been thinking about this statement all week. And I find it very unsettling. The more I analyze my thoughts, the more I feel like Charlton Heston discovering that Soylent Green is actually dead people. *THIS is what I've been feeding myself??*

The only conclusion I can draw is that by and large, I am a liar. Unless I am very intentional, the steady stream of self-talk running through my mind on a daily basis is unbiblical. Especially when it comes to parenting. As a result, I often feel discouraged, afraid, and insecure as a mom. Here are the two biggest lies I believe:

Lie #1: My children are a reflection of my worth and identity.
Believing this lie is the surest way to climb on a rollercoaster and never get off. I know I believe this lie when I ricochet between pride and despair depending on how my children behave. Even worse, this lie produces selfish parenting. I'm driven to control my kids because my identity is riding on their behavior. At the end of the day, I'm not motivated by love for them, but love for myself.

And here's a sad thought—how are we going to counsel our child through *his* identity crisis when *our* identity is wrapped up in *his* identity? No kid needs a mom who falls apart every time he struggles. He needs a mom who's steadfast because her hope is in the Lord. Only then can she lead, counsel, and be a model for him.

Lie #2: The greatest determining factor in my child's spiritual growth is my performance as a parent.
If lie #1 leads to selfish parenting, I think this lie leads to fearful parenting. And boy is this one deeply rooted in my heart. It's why I constantly feel guilty for turning on Curious George instead of reading the girls a Bible story. It's why I pat myself on the back when we do a biblically-integrated craft or have a spiritual "discussion." It's why I resent the fact that ungodly parents can raise godly children, and godly parents can raise ungodly children. If I were completely honest, I'd admit that I want a guarantee. I want to know that if I do X-Y-Z, then my children will grow up to love and worship the Lord whole-heartedly.

But the Bible teaches that salvation has and always will be in the hands of the Lord. John 6:44 says, "No one can come to Me unless the Father who sent Me draws him." Although we're called to spiritually train our children, at the end of the day *Jesus* saves. Not Bible stories and sheep crafts.

Rather than be scared by this, I am choosing to be freed by it. Because the sweet truth is, *nobody is more passionate about my children's spiritual growth, or more capable of producing it then Jesus Christ.*

I wonder, what would change in our lives if we started telling ourselves the Truth about *everything*? Not just parenting, but the truth about our future, the truth about our status before God, the truth about our acceptance and forgiveness and hope for change? What if we told ourselves the truth about the value in all the menial things we do all day? The truth about God's ever-present grace?

What if we started by simply *listening* to our thoughts? By thinking about what we're thinking about. And then choosing to think in a more Christ-centered way. My guess is that you and I would be a lot more joyful, a lot less fearful, and a lot more fun to be around.

How Mama Bear Hurts Her Family

I've never loved the "Mama Bear" analogy. When I think of "Mama Bears," I picture moms who bite teachers' heads off, and elbow their way through crowds so their kids can get the best seat at story time. I'd much rather be a Mama Swan, peacefully gliding through life with all my little cygnets in a row. But I'm not. I'm the swan-faced mom with the heart of a grizzly.

The truth is you don't have to be loud and obnoxious to be a Mama Bear. You just have to care *too much* about the well-being of your family. You have to idolize it. To bow down and worship it, so that if anyone in your household isn't okay, nothing's okay. You see, the thing about Mama Bears is that deep down, we long to control our universe so that we can protect the people we love. If we're Christians, on some level we know this is impossible. But that doesn't stop us from trying. How *can* we stop trying? Then things might *really* fall apart. So we spin our wheels endlessly, longing for that moment when we can take a deep breath and say, "Life is good. Nobody's in the hospital. Nobody's failing fourth grade. Nobody's miserable at work." Of course, this kind of peace is fragile as an eggshell. It's like building your home on a foundation of toothpicks.

And boy is it exhausting. I knew there would be a lot of work in becoming a wife and mom; I just didn't realize how much of it would be done on the inside instead of the outside. The more people we add to our family, the more my heart has to carry. Worry, concern, love, joy, pain, affection, fear. I don't even want a hamster, because I don't have the emotional capacity to care for one more living thing! There are days when my husband walks through the door with a heavy expression on his face, and I want to hold up a hand and say, "I'm sorry!! The anxiety meter has reached maximum capacity. Put one more burden on my plate and I will drop dead right here in the kitchen! Then you'll have to finish cooking." Instead I usually opt for the quick-fix: "What's wrong? Just tell me. Tell me now." *Maybe I can slap some gospel truth on this one real fast and check it off the list before the chicken burns.*

But it doesn't work that way for one simple reason. I'm not Jesus. All my outward attempts to "fix" our universe are just that—outward attempts. They're the toothpicks straining under the weight of the house that will always crush them flat. I still remember the day Clint looked at me and said, "Can you just let me be *not okay*? Can you just love me when I'm not happy?"

But if you're *not okay, then* I'm *not okay*, I thought. And just like that, I finally got it. Wanting him to be okay was never really about him. It was always about me. I didn't want to abide with him in a season of long-suffering. I wanted it over. Fixed. So that *I* could go back to being happy. I've known that Mama Bears (like me) are protective and controlling. But this was the first time I realized we're also selfish. So selfish, in fact, that we're willing to short-circuit what God wants to do in someone's life, just so we don't have to endure the discomfort of watching it.

When little Susie has no friends at school, Mama Bears (like me) don't want to walk the long, painful road of teaching her to trust Jesus. We just want to make the heartache *go away.* We want to throw a block party and invite every 5-year-old in Georgia. But what if God destined this to be the first time little Susie turned to Jesus with a real problem? What if this heartache sets the stage for her first experience of believing God and seeing Him act on her behalf? Isn't that worth a little suffering? For Susie...*and* for Mama Bear?

But the only way we will become the kind of woman with the ability to *abide* instead of *fix,* is if we abide in Christ. David once sang, "God is our refuge and strength, an ever-present help in trouble. Therefore we will not fear, though the earth give way and the mountains fall into the heart of the sea."[17] Don't you *long* to have such assurance on the day your private mountains fall into the heart of the sea? On the day your husband loses his job? Or the pediatrician says you need to see a specialist? Or your grown child calls to tell you she's getting a divorce?

I guarantee you, Mama Bear longs for it. Because she understands life on the other side. She lives in the house built on sand, and even on the good days, she fears it's sinking. I wish I could say it's easy to pick up that house and plop it down on the Solid Rock of Christ. I wish it was a one-time thing. But it's not. It is a moment-by-moment choice to yield and to trust. Then, and only then, can we minister to our families with the sort of love that says, "Come as you are, messy and in pain. I will abide with you. As long as it takes."

Why the Vaccination Debate is So Nasty (And Why It Ought Not Be)

Of all the Mommy-War debates, I can think of few that are as emotionally charged as the war over vaccines. Does that make me want to avoid the topic? Only like a nuclear missile. Unfortunately, (like a nuclear missile) that also makes it so important. My goal is not to re-hash the hundreds of arguments for or against vaccines. Rather, my goal is to answer a simple question: As Christian mothers, how should we approach this sensitive and volatile topic personally, among friends and strangers, and in our social media testimony?

When I set out to answer this question, I started by asking myself *why* the vaccination debate is so heated. I think there are three predominant factors. First, it involves **personal heartache**. Many (if not the majority of) mothers who choose not to vaccinate have what they would call a "vaccine-injured child." They truly believe vaccinations have had adverse effects on their child. In some cases, the conditions their children face are extreme, lifelong, and even deadly. Whether or not vaccines are to blame for these conditions, the point is these moms (who are not stupid, nor short on research) truly believe they are. My children are vaccinated, and I have not experienced adverse side effects. However, I can imagine how outraged, confused, and afraid I would feel if I thought my kids were suffering because a doctor told me to do something that I believed hurt them.

But unfortunately, this issue is also emotionally charged because it has **communal implications.** Whether or not you believe in "herd immunity," our society still functions in support of it. In other words, our government and medical professionals believe immunizations are in the best interest of society at large. That's why you're still required to present an immunization record at kindergarten open house. It's why doctors talk about mutations of previously eradicated diseases emerging as the anti-vaccination movement grows. Whether or not you agree, you can understand why vaccinating parents find this scary. Ironically, it's the exact same fear non-vaccinating parents feel—the fear that something poses a threat to our children.

The final reason I think the debate is so heated is because it's a **high stakes** issue. I've seen articles and videos that claim infants have died from adverse reactions to vaccinations. On the flip side, I've talked to doctors who claim they've seen infants and children die from vaccine-preventable diseases. Any way you look at it, fear, suffering, and the desire to protect our children are the primary emotions driving the war over vaccines. Our fleshly instinct is to respond to these emotions with all manner of ungodliness. Both sides are guilty. *(See my table for a brief synopsis of sentiments I've heard and read.)*

The problem isn't that we have an opinion on this issue. It's not even that our opinion is bound to differ with someone else's. The problem lies in how *much* we value our opinion. Biblically, I believe Christian moms are free to stand on either side of the debate. I don't believe there is anything inherently sinful about vaccinating or not vaccinating your children, so long as you are submitted to God and motivated by love for Him and your kids. But, it *is* sinful to elevate this issue above Christ.

	Anti-Vaccines	**Pro-Vaccines**
Pride and Condescension	"I love my babies too much to put such-and-such chemicals into them."	"I love my babies too much to put them at risk for preventable diseases."
Hatred	"I hope your kids end up injured by a vaccine so you change your tune!"	"I hope your kids catch a disease and die!"
Judgment	"Parents who vaccinate are un-researched, blind followers."	"Parents who don't vaccinate ought to be jailed for child abuse."
Selfishness	"This isn't about *your* children. I'm not thinking about your children at all! This is about *my* children."	"I don't care what your story is, if your kid isn't vaccinated, keep him away from *my* kid!"

Before you assume you're not guilty of this, here are some hard questions I've had to ask myself: *Does thinking (or reading) about this issue ever evoke feelings of hatred or judgment within me? Has it ever made me wish suffering on someone else? Do my words and lifestyle reflect that I'm more passionate about this topic than I am about the gospel? Does it consume my thoughts or control my emotions? When others think of me, is this issue one of the first things they think of?*

Yes, this is a high stakes issue. But when it comes to how we interact with it, there is something **even greater** at stake: our testimony to a watching world. Vaccinations impact this life, but our testimony for Christ impacts eternity. How foolish we would be to sacrifice something of eternal value for the sake of an earthly cause! Am I saying it's wrong to share your opinion on vaccinations? Of course not. But if you value your opinion to the point that it causes you to sin against others (in thought, word, or action), then for you this issue has become an idol. In essence, you are more devoted to it than you are to the mandates of Christ.

Let me be the first to admit, I'm on the guilty side of this reality. This issue has stirred arrogance, judgment, and anxiety in my heart and mind. The only way I'm dethroning it in my life, is by fighting fear with the true, biblical antidote. The fact is, the solution for fear and suffering has never been found in "winning" the external war. You can't get rid of the turmoil in your heart by converting the world, one tweet at a time, toward or against vaccinations. The only true antidote is faith. If we truly *believe* that all the days ordained for our children are written in God's book,[18] that He alone is the author of their lives, wiser than any parent and stronger than any threat, I believe it would change the way we approach this debate.

I don't know about you, but I don't want to be the mom who hopes other kids suffer because their mother doesn't agree with me. I don't want to be the mom who turns unbelievers off to the gospel because of my testimony over a spiritually gray issue. Like the Psalmist, I want to be the kind of mom who says, "The Lord is the stronghold of my life—of whom (or what) shall I be afraid?" The kind of mom whose heart, passion, and legacy cry out:

> One thing I ask of the Lord, this is what I seek: that I may dwell in the house of the Lord all the days of my life, to gaze upon the beauty of the Lord and to seek him in his temple.[19]

Only then, will I be able to take a stance on this issue with love, humility, freedom, and peace.

Secrets of a Sinful Mom

Today is Mother's Day and I am thankful for many things. The way my baby sticks her cutest-feet-in-the-universe right in my face whenever she sees nail polish. The adoration of a toddler who's seen me at my worst and for some reason still wants to be just like me. My own mother, who makes me brave. The fact that I married a man who's sensitive enough to show me his heart, but strong enough to take care of mine.

I am thankful for Nutella, and the strangers in the grocery store who don't stare when my kids throw a tantrum, and the miracle of instant streaming. I'm thankful for my bed, and the inventor of sweat pants, and frozen yogurt you can pretend is good for you. For older women who don't panic when I tell them my problems, and young moms who walk alongside me, and single girlfriends who still like to talk about boys.

But of all the things I am grateful for this Mother's Day, most of all, I am grateful for grace. Sometimes I think about "high school Jeanne"—who had a heart full of passion, a head full of idealism, and seldom lost her temper—and I wonder where on earth she's gone. I wonder how I went from daydreaming about impacting the world for Christ, to fantasizing about a minivan with a conveyor belt that can transport snacks to the back seat.

The truth is I have never seen the depth of my own sinfulness and unworthiness with as painful clarity as I've seen it in the last few years. Of course it's always been there, I've just never been "squeezed" enough to let it spew out quite so badly. Let's be honest, "high school Jeanne" didn't have children who loved to crawl all over her, and test the boundaries, and stick tiny objects into the DVD player. Instead, she had oodles of free time and a mom who did her laundry.

But here's the amazing thing about seeing how incredibly awful you actually are. **It makes *grace* look BIGGER than it's ever looked before.** When you have a snail-high view of your own righteousness, somehow it finally sinks in that you didn't reach past this tiny gap, up into the presence of God. Instead, He reached down, down, down, down, down to you. The gap was gigantic—infinite. Which means *the grace is gigantic. Infinite.* Now *that* is reason to rejoice! That is cause to smile, and celebrate, and throw your hands up high in worship!

The more I decrease in my own eyes, the more my Savior increases. And the more I put my hope in Him, the less I have to prove. I am a weak and sinful mother. But I have a GREAT and MIGHTY God, who loves me with all His heart. Today, more than anything, that is what I'm grateful for. Until I am old and gray, that will be the joy of my heart and the song of my life.

Peanut Butter Princess

Peanut Butter Princess
with sticky-icky hands,
and 27 crowns
and twice as many fans!
Put on plastic heels,
clatter through the house,
smear peanut butter fingers
on Mommy's satin blouse.
Dance on Daddy's head
at the crack of dawn,
put lipstick on your eyebrows,
wave your hotdog wand!
And I will wear a tutu
and laugh until I cry;
My Peanut Butter Princess,
I'll love you 'til I die.

Can You Really Raise a Child with an Unbiased Worldview?

The notion of raising a child with an "unbiased worldview" is growing increasingly popular. Parents want to raise children who are "free to find their own spirituality" without parental bias. Conversely, attempting to raise a child with a biblical worldview seems to be going the way of pleated pants and flip phones. Not only is it unpopular, it's often viewed as arrogant, controlling, and close-minded. Parents are seen as "imposing their worldview" upon their children, even "brainwashing" them.

The issue is so loaded that I've heard Christian parents question whether or not they should raise their children spiritually "neutral." It just seems so intolerant, even manipulative, to teach an impressionable young child that God is real. That God created her in His own image for His own glory. That she inherited a sin nature from Adam. And that God loves her so passionately that He Himself died in her place to save her.

But here's the bottom line: ***every parent raises their child with a biased worldview.*** We are *constantly* teaching our children how to view the world, whether we "mean to" or not. Every time they see us rejoice or get angry, we are teaching them something about what we value. The fact that you probably choose to raise your children in a home, with food and clothing *teaches* them that you find those things important. And if you get down on one knee and tell them that they can determine who God is for themselves, or that they can accept or reject any religion with no consequences, you are *not raising them spiritually neutral.* You are raising them with a very particular, biased worldview.

Thus the question isn't *should* we influence our children's worldview. Like it or not, we're already doing that. The real question is *how* should we influence it? If you are a believer, the Bible gives you an answer. In Deuteronomy 6:6-7, after exhorting the Israelites to love the One True God with their whole hearts, Moses issues a mighty charge:

> And these words...shall be on your heart. You shall *teach them diligently to your children*, and shall talk of them when you sit in your house, and when you walk by the way, and when you lie down, and when you rise.

Clearly Christians are to be intentional about raising their children in the discipline and instruction of the Lord,[20] recognizing that only God has the power to save. Fulfilling this biblical mandate is *loving*, not controlling. Consider this: you and I teach our children countless things from the moment they're born. We teach them that the bump below their eyes is called a "nose" and that cows say "moo." Nobody calls us close-minded or accuses us of "brainwashing" when we do this. Inherently, they recognize our teaching as truth. So dear Christian, if you really believe Christ's claims are as *true* and *real* as the nose on your daughter's face, how could you *not* teach them to her? How could you withhold the very truth that has the power to save her soul on the grounds of allowing her the freedom to "find her own way"? If you're willing to teach her that there's a nose on her face, be willing to teach her the truths that matter so much more than that.

If you don't believe the claims of Christ, then I understand why you wouldn't teach them to your children. I don't judge you for influencing your child according to your personal beliefs. But I do urge you not to judge Christians for doing the same thing, and not to deceive yourself into believing you are raising your child neutrally.

Perhaps as you read this, you don't know what you think of God. Perhaps you've been disappointed by Him, confused by Him, or simply feel indifferent to Him. Regardless of where you are on your journey with God, I *wholeheartedly believe* He loves you more than you could ever fathom and longs to have a relationship with you. No matter what you've done or what's been done to you, He is faithful and trustworthy. He is capable of bringing beauty from ashes, of restoring what's been lost, and of making all things new in Christ.[21]

Why Having More Babies Isn't as Crazy as You May Think

The first time a kind stranger peeked at my newborn baby and gushed, "Oh honey, treasure every second!" I almost burst into tears. Not because I was so touched, but because I was *so tired.* We were standing at the entrance to the mall—me, my baby, and my Shamu-sized postpartum belly—all three of us staring at this sweet woman with her abounding supply of freedom.

I wanted to say, "I'll try! I'll try to treasure every second, and *you* try to treasure every second of the eight hours of uninterrupted sleep you're going to get tonight. And treasure every second you're going to roam this mall in total freedom, buying clothes that will fit your skinny waist, and shirts that aren't breastfeeding accessible. And while you're at it, treasure all the discretionary time you'll have in the next decade while I watch the Backyardigans, and take temperatures, and settle fights, and pretend to be a human jungle gym, and birth more babies, and clean puke off my clothes." Instead I just smiled and waddled off—me, baby, and Shamu. That was round one for me. My very first baby. And boy, was the learning curve *steep.*

Two weeks ago I gave birth to baby number three. My little Lila Jeanne. She arrived three weeks early, in such a massive hurry that despite having two previous C-sections, I delivered her naturally with no drugs...and a whole lot of screaming! It was the first time I experienced a baby being laid on my chest the moment she was born. Later, the midwife told me she would never forget the look on my face. It wasn't pretty or serene (Clint snapped a picture, so I know!) It was a look of complete shock. Somewhere in the midst of all the pain and hysteria, I had completely forgotten I would get a baby out of this ordeal. My mom (who thought this one might be a boy, despite the ultrasound's verdict) asked me later if it registered that she really was a girl. I told her that in that moment I wouldn't have cared if she was a monkey. I held my little baby as they stitched me up, and I never felt more comforted in all my life. I didn't examine her, or talk to her, or try to nurse her...I just *abided* with her, quietly knowing that she and I together had done something extraordinary. We each went on a journey—scary and unknown—and we met in the middle.

This time, if a kind stranger tells me to treasure every second, I think I *will* burst into tears. Not because of my lost figure or freedom, but because I so ardently understand that the seconds truly are numbered. They are grains of sand slipping through the hourglass, never to be returned. That's the funny thing about motherhood. You start off with so little on your plate, and it feels like you're absolutely drowning. And yet the more you add, the more joyful it becomes. Because somewhere in between adding more babies, and more diapers, and more laundry, you also add more perspective. You realize there are worse things than a long night, and reflux really does pass, and tiny toes don't stay tiny forever. You know cribs turn into beds, and strollers turn into bikes, and the chubby cheeks making fish faces today will be wearing your makeup tomorrow.

And so, in these past two weeks, as I *treasure every second,* one verse keeps coming to my mind: "Isaac brought her into the tent of his mother Sarah, and he married Rebekah. So she became his wife, and he loved her; and Isaac was comforted after his mother's death."[22]

Is it busy and hectic and messy having three children? You bet! Have I gone to bed at 8pm every night this week? Yes I have! But this time around, the *baby* isn't the exhausting, overwhelming part. In the midst of all the scheduling, and carpooling, and cleaning, the baby is my Rebekah. She is the *comfort* in the chaos.

Welcome to the world, darling. We love you.

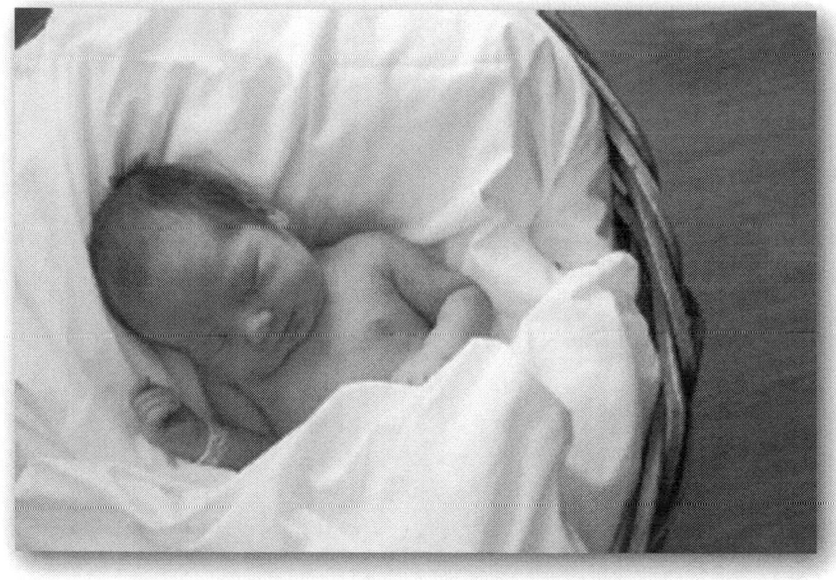

Mom vs. Mom: The War I Didn't See Coming

Before I ever had a single child, I knew that one day I would wage war with an enemy who sought their hearts and souls. I anticipated battles ahead, knowing my children would test and defy me. But I never anticipated the Mommy wars. I think I watched part of an Oprah episode years ago on competitive moms, but that was about it. I didn't give it a second thought. Not until I joined the club.

Let me begin by saying, the Mommy Club is a beautiful place. The moment you join, you find within your heart an unexpectedly raw capacity for love. All at once, you are a protector, a nurturer, a defender of innocence, a storyteller, an imagination factory, a kisser of boo-boos, and a cheerleader forever. Even on the scrape-me-off-the-floor-with-a-spatula days, you are being sanctified and learning to see God's grace in a brand new light.

But I'll be honest, there's one aspect of membership I don't like to talk about. It's the insecurity that bloomed inside of me somewhere along the journey. I felt it the first time I didn't know how to soothe my own baby. The first time I couldn't get her to eat her green bean goo. The first time she wandered out of my sight in public. I don't know exactly when the quiet voice began to whisper, *do you even know what you're doing?* But I do know that initial thought was just a stone's throw away from this one: *That mom sure looks like* she *knows what she's doing.* And then there was the really quiet thought that always buried itself in a place I would never share with anyone: *Maybe she's a better mom than you.*

Here's my humble opinion: I think that thought is the deceptive heartbeat behind all the mommy wars. I think deep down many of us are just a little bit afraid that someone else is doing a better job at this whole thing than we are. We see All-Natural-Organic Mom who tills her own grains in the backyard, and Educational-Crafty Mom whose newborn knows sign language, and Just-Stepped-Out-of-a-Magazine Mom with super cute clothes and baby Gap model babies...and we cannot help but notice all the ways we fall short. So we resort to one of two measures, the first being imitation.

Maybe if I can just be like Super-Fit-and-Sporty Mom with16% body fat and color-coordinated Nike outfits, or Ultra-Organized Mom, or Über-Sweet-and-Godly Mom... The problem is we quickly realize we cannot be *all* of them *all* the time. The moment we pop on All-Natural-Organic Mom's hat, we bump into Crafty Mom whose kids have sculpted a miniature Parthenon over the weekend, and we realize *our kids* have watched twenty hours of television so we could make Larabars from scratch. And even if by some *miracle* we can get Healthy Mom jiving with Educational Mom, when we drop off our kids at preschool we'll immediately notice that Just-Stepped-Out-of-a-Magazine Mom isn't sporting a crumpled T-shirt with craft glue in her hair. (And don't even get me started on what Coupon Mom might think if she saw how much we spent on groceries last week!)

Once we realize we can't be all of them, we resort to option number two: judgment. Of course, this is rarely blatant. I don't tell Sporty Mom I think she spends too much time at the gym, I tell *myself* Sporty Mom spends too much time at the gym. I tell myself it's okay my abs don't look like hers because she's probably not nearly as godly as I am. I tell myself it's okay I don't look as put together as Just-Stepped-Out-of-a-Magazine Mom because she probably spends too much money on clothes anyway. On and on, I tell myself whatever I think I need to hear to stanch the fear that I don't measure up.

A few times I have seen the mommy wars go viral. Moms screaming at each other on television. A Facebook feed that erupts. A hateful gossip fest. Here is my theory: I picture the hearts of moms across the world like a really dry forest, the kind that people warn you not to strike a match in. They are dry because they're insecure and aching. They are exhausted and spent. They are longing to hear that they're doing a good job, and what's more to *feel* like they're doing a good job. But because rest and truth and hope can be so hard won, these dry hearts are hazardous. Flick a spark in their direction and the whole forest can go up in flames.

But what if the hearts of moms were *watered?* Not sprinkled every now and then, but watered all the way down to their roots. What if we knew in the core of our being, that *we don't have to measure up?* What if we knew that Jesus Christ *loves* and *accepts* us just as we are? That He is passionate about our children and will walk beside us, in all our shortcomings, to make us the kind of mom we need to be. What if we could quit judging Skinny Mom or Healthy Mom or Crafty Mom and instead see them as Real-Human Mom in need of love and encouragement just like us? Then maybe the next time someone suggests you try her organic Ak-Mak crackers or mentions that she just finished a triathlon, you can smile genuinely because you may have no idea what an Ak-Mak cracker is, but you know who *you* are. Accepted. Redeemed. Treasured. One who has been born again to a living hope and an imperishable inheritance.[23]

What do you say, Mom? How would you like to be Imperfect-Completely-Loved-Free-in-Jesus Mom? How would you like to be Don't-Need-to-Play-the-Games Mom? Capable-of-Genuinely-Loving-Others Mom? Guess what? That is *exactly* what Jesus died to offer you. Initially when I started thinking about this topic, I wanted to encourage you by telling you all the things I myself long to hear—that you're doing a great job, you're the best mom ever, everything's going to be awesome for you. But instead, I want to encourage you by telling you something far better; whether you're doing a great job or not, Jesus loves you. You don't have to be the best mom ever, Jesus accepts you. And when everything's *not* awesome, you always have hope in Jesus.

Homemaker

"THEOLOGY IS FOR HOMEMAKERS WHO NEED TO KNOW WHO GOD IS, WHO THEY ARE, AND WHAT THIS MUNDANE LIFE IS ALL ABOUT."

Gloria Furman, *Glimpses of Grace*

Running a Home While Running on Empty

For almost three years in between ministry positions, my husband managed a local car wash company. One hot summer afternoon, he strode through the front door and announced that he had a surprise. He pulled a tiny princess coloring book out of his pocket and handed it to Aubrey. Sheer ecstasy erupted. She danced in circles, hugged him at least ten times, and profusely thanked him. Then she sat down and colored every single page.

While she was occupied, I turned to him and asked, "Where did you get it?"

"The trashcan," he replied.

It still makes me laugh. I can picture her intently bent over each picture, carefully coloring, while Clint and I smile in the kitchen.

Sometimes when I feel truly depleted, I think about Aubrey and her coloring book, and I wonder how much of what I treasure in my life is actually garbage. I've never been physically anorexic, but there are spells when I feel spiritually anorexic. I feast on all sorts of garbage—entertainment, distractions, idols, my own ability to perform—everything but Jesus. As a result, I'm crammed to the gills and starving just the same. And somehow in this state, I manage to keep going for a really long time. After all, the dishes always need washing, the kids always need feeding, and the floors always need sweeping. So I truck along like the Energizer Bunny, ignoring all the signs of spiritual starvation, until one day the battery of my own effort finally runs dry. Something touches this raw, cavernous hunger in my soul for Jesus, and before I know it, I'm crying and I'm not even sure why.

It's ironic isn't it? God is ever present; the feast of His presence lies before us, and we pass the days munching on cocktail peanuts. And we wonder why we're so hungry. But how do we change? How do we find fulfillment in Christ amid the daily drudgery? These two principles are helping me more than any other:

Practicing the Presence of Christ

Running a home is incredibly monotonous. Not only are the tasks menial, few ever remain "finished," which can make you feel a little like Sisyphus endlessly rolling the rock (or laundry basket) uphill. But what if we changed our perspective to recognize the vast reward in the "doing" rather than the "accomplishing"? Unlike the world, Christ does not ask us to achieve. He asks us to be faithful. Thus, as Oswald Chambers writes, "drudgery is the touchstone of character."[24] Look at Christ Himself, who washed the disciples' feet. Can you picture Him changing diapers with great love and joy? I can, because no calling from the Father was ever too menial for Jesus. He came to serve, to love the least of these, and to do it with or without the praise of men. How then can I refuse to do the same for Him? Brother Lawrence who lived out his days as a kitchen aide in a monastery, wrote:

> I turn the cake that is frying on the pan for love of him, and that done, if there is nothing else to call me, I prostrate myself in worship before him, who has given me grace to work; afterwards I rise happier than a king. It is enough for me to pick up but a straw from the ground for the love of God.[25]

Like Brother Lawrence, you and I can practice the presence of Christ every time we wipe Desitin on a rash-y bottom, and rise happier than a king! And therein lies the secret to running a home with joy and purpose. We are doing all things as an act of love and worship for *Him.*

Resting in the Presence of Christ

I find that practicing the presence of Christ in the hectic chores of the day is always easier when I spend quiet moments resting in Him. Sometimes these moments come first thing in the morning, sometimes during nap time, and sometimes last in the day. Either way, they are crucial because these are the moments when I feast. I lay all my longings before Him, and I am overcome by His intense love for me despite my unworthiness. To quote *The Jesus Storybook Bible,* His love makes me lovely. His love makes *my life* lovely.[26]

At times I'm tempted to skip these moments with God for love of a lesser idol, and at times I'm tempted to fulfill them dutifully and rigidly like a slave. I know both attitudes must break His heart. Yet graciously, every time I come to Him, whether for love of Him or love of myself, He meets me. At the height of my joy, He meets me. In the pit of my sorrow, He meets me. In the thick of my drudgery, He meets me.

Surely, you and I don't have to run on empty! Not with a God like this. We can run by His power and grace. We can run through the happiness, through the failure, and through the ten million dirty diapers ahead. We can run in the very presence of Christ.

The House that Cleans Itself

The first time I saw these five words on the cover of a book they looked as tantalizing as a cream-filled doughnut. If there's one idol I've battled for years, it's the idol of wanting a perfectly tidy home. For some reason my mom has always had this innate, Mary Poppins-like ability to create order out of chaos. As a result I grew up in a beautifully organized home that ran like a well-oiled machine. And then I got married, moved into my own little house, and made two startling realizations: keeping an entire house clean is crazy hard, and I am not my mother. Suffice to say it didn't get any easier when I added three children and 10,000 Barbie dolls. Plus accessories.

Over the years I've felt all sorts of things when it comes to housekeeping—guilt, frustration, the desire to curl up in the closet and cry. Which is why I was so taken aback to read this statement in Mindy Starns Clark's book:

> The startling truth is that *cleaning really shouldn't have any emotional component at all.* It's not an emotional subject. It's just a necessary set of tasks. If the thought of cleaning house evokes any [strong] emotion…it's time to unpack that baggage and see what's in there. It's making housekeeping, which is just a necessary part of life, much more difficult than it needs to be.[27]

Right off the bat this helped me make it through the rest of Clark's book, because let me just warn you, the woman is *detailed.* But if you can let go of the emotional component, you're free to apply the principles you like and not feel guilty for ignoring the ones that are beyond your stamina. That being said, here are my three favorite principles from her book (re-phrased in my own words):

Don't just tidy, figure out what's causing the mess and problem-solve.

To do this, you have to analyze the way mess accumulates in your particular home. For instance, there's always a pile of books on the end table in our den, usually dirty socks on the floor, and a huge (amazingly comfortable) blue chair that's crusted over with sticky handprints. Normally I ignore the books, take the socks to the laundry room, and wash the blue slip cover every few weeks. Okay, months. After thinking like a problem-solver, I designated a basket for the books we're currently reading, stowed a hamper discreetly in the den, and made a new rule—no one under twenty-five gets to eat in the blue chair! By the time I problem-solved my way through the whole house, the mess had begun to reduce itself rapidly.

Get rid of as MUCH as possible.

Clark taught me to view *every single object* in my house as owning a piece of my time. Furniture, paper clips, toys, that monogrammed bridesmaid gift in the attic—*everything.* The question you have to ask is: Is this object *worth* the time it takes to clean it, dust it, straighten it, pick it up, pack it, and move it? The simple truth is, the less you have, the easier it is to maintain order.

Create a "launching pad" and eliminate "rabbit trails." Two of the most common ways mess accumulates is in the entryway of your home and in the pursuit of what Clark calls "rabbit trails." A rabbit trail is any activity you frequently embark upon that requires supplies from around the house. For instance, I store wrapping paper in the upstairs guest bedroom closet, simply because there's *room* for it there. But of course, the tape and scissors are downstairs in the study, and I actually wrap gifts on the dining room table. Once I've gathered all the supplies and wrapped my gifts, what's the likelihood that I will put them all back where they belong before next Christmas? Clark's solution is to set up "stations" wherever the task is accomplished. In my case, there should be a large container with all the supplies necessary to wrap presents stored out of sight somewhere in the dining room.

To help out your entryway, Clark suggests a "launching pad"—a cabinet, bookcase, closet, or shelving unit somewhere near the main entryway that holds all the items you enter and exit with on a regular basis, like your purse, keys, or sunglasses. If your kids are school-aged, they can each have their own bin in the launching pad to hold things like backpacks and library books. This is a fast way to stop the clutter as it comes in the door, and to keep from losing important items.

All in all, I loved the improvements Clark's book brought to our home. If you have the time and energy, I'd recommend giving her system a shot. Take it with a grain of salt, use what you like, ignore what you don't, and thank God for the gift of a home—messy, clean, calm, and crazy.

Eating to Honor God

A few months after the documentary *Forks Over Knives* hit Netflix, my husband talked me into watching it. Stifling a groan and about twenty-six yawns, I settled in for the foodie film. If you're unfamiliar with it, the movie uses scientific and medical research to champion a Vegan lifestyle. It underscores the link between processed, animal-based foods and cancer, heart disease, diabetes, and other illnesses. About thirty minutes in, Clint was clutching his heart, certain it would stop beating at any moment.

By the time the credits rolled, he was inspired: "Let's do it!" I was woebegone. As the family chef, the thought of re-structuring our entire diet was not only daunting, but depressing. But I couldn't shake the guilt I felt, especially toward my children. *If I know that highly-processed foods are so unhealthy for my little ones, why do I still hand them out?* "Convenience" hardly seemed a suitable answer when their health was at stake. So, I resolved to take baby steps toward healthier eating. For several months I struggled along, until it finally dawned on me to ask the question, "What does the *Bible* say about eating?"

The moment I started to explore the topic, I grew encouraged. The ocean of fad diets and whole-food-blogging-gurus slowly gave way to a stable and steady shore, one that promised to guide me with truth, not trends. In the end, I narrowed my study to six principles, which I hoped would give me a framework for feeding my family.

WE ARE CALLED TO EAT FOR GOD'S GLORY.

The first thing I saw is that eating to honor God is a biblical mandate. I Corinthians 10:31 says, "So, whether you eat or drink, or whatever you do, do all to the glory of God." As Christians, everything related to food—from what we eat to the attitude we have while preparing it—-should glorify God.

WE ARE CALLED TO BE FREE FROM LEGALISM.

In the Old Testament, there were "unclean" foods that Jews were forbidden to eat. Then, in Acts 10:9-16, Peter had a vision in which God declared the unclean food, "clean," telling Peter to "Rise, kill, and eat." Symbolically, God was preparing Peter to receive Gentiles into the faith, declaring that He has made them "clean." As believers in Christ, there is no longer any food forbidden to us. We do not have to plan our weekly menu enslaved by legalism. Or as I like to think of it, I don't have to feel guilty for letting Papa John cook now and then. According to Galatians 5, I have been set free and called to freedom, therefore I don't want my philosophy of eating to be enslaving.

WE ARE CALLED TO BE FAITHFUL STEWARDS OF OUR BODIES.

Although we are permitted to eat anything, the Bible reminds us that our "body is a temple of the Holy Spirit" and we are to present it as a "living sacrifice, holy and acceptable to God" which is an act of *worship*.[28] Exercising wisdom and self-control in eating demonstrates faithful stewardship. This is an especially serious responsibility for parents of small children, because they are entirely dependent on us to feed them. They can't make a grocery list, go to the store, and buy healthy foods. They eat what they are given. Therefore, *we* are accountable as stewards of their bodies. *(Yikes, I know! My thoughts exactly.)*

We are called to humility.

Personally, I think the subject of food is particularly sensitive for women. It's a tender topic for numerous reasons: it's tied to our abilities as a homemaker, our body image, our parenting style, our organization and planning (or lack thereof). And because of this, it can become a source of pride for those who make it their pedestal. But clearly God opposes both pride and judgment.[29] So as we create our philosophy of eating, let's remember that we can be an all-natural, organic superstar, but if we harbor a spirit of pride, we're losing on the front that really counts.

We are called to seek comfort, refuge, and satisfaction in God alone.

We must examine our *motives* for eating. Repeatedly the Bible speaks of God being our only true refuge and comfort.[30] Yet it is tempting to use food as a false refuge, seeking the comfort of a warm brownie... or eight. At the same time, we can sin in the opposite direction by seeking satisfaction through *not eating.* So the question is *why am I making these food choices?* Am I doing it to honor God, or to fill the empty corners of my heart? To honor God, or to seek a worldly self-image? To honor God, or because I am in bondage to fear of disease?

We are called to serve one another.

Finally, we must take a brief stop at the home of the Proverbs 31 woman, who "rises while it is yet night and provides food for her household." What a gal. One of the things I dislike the most about myself is that when I'm preparing food I often morph into this "angry-bear-get-out-of-my-way-I'm-COOKING!" version of myself. The thought of this woman (with no stove, dishwasher, or microwave) rising while it is still night to prepare food is deeply challenging. Here is a woman who embraces cooking as service to her family and her God. If you've ever been around a woman like this, you know how beautiful it is. My mother-in-law is one such woman, and on many pre-holiday occasions I have quietly chopped vegetables alongside her and marveled at her whole-hearted, unselfish delight in ministering to her family via the humble avenue of food-preparation.

Are you beginning to see the beautiful balance inherent in God's Word? Imagine how "Momville" might change if we planned our menus, and simmered our sauces, and tweeted our thoughts with these principles in mind. Imagine how *you* might change. More conviction, less guilt. More satisfaction, less frustration. More joy, less judgment. Now there's a recipe for a happy kitchen, and a sweet-smelling soul to go with it.

8 Ways to Cultivate a More Restful Home

When I think of my home, there are so many adjectives that are important to me: orderly, attractive, efficient. But when I think about the people within my home, one adjective rises above all the others: *restful.* Oh how I would love for my husband and children to describe their home as the most restful place on earth. A place where they can kick off their shoes and breathe. To me, creating a home like this would be one of the greatest gifts I could give them. Lately, I've been asking myself *how* I could make our home more restful. Here are some thoughts from someone who still has a long way to go.

MAKE REST AND REFRESHMENT A PERSONAL PRIORITY.

Nobody wants an anemic for a blood donor. Sure, I could wake up running and not pause for breath until bedtime, but I'd probably look more like Medusa than Martha Stewart. And honestly, the first to suffer would be my family. So how do I make time for rest? It depends on the season. Right now, with three young children, I've found two practical windows for rest: during the baby's afternoon nap, and in the evening when the kids are in bed. *Look at your schedule. Where could you allot some time for personal rest?*

Recognize that there's a hierarchy to rest.

Not all restful activities are created equally. Watching thirteen movies in a row may be restful, but not rejuvenating or nourishing. If we want *lasting* rest, the Bible says it only comes in a Person.[31] I don't think that means there's no room for personal hobbies, it just means those forms of rest shouldn't trump the most important form. *How are you using your free time? Is it providing lasting rest?*

Enforce a consistent bedtime for the kids.

From the moment our kids exited the womb, we started putting them to bed at 7pm. Of course it took time to get them used to the routine, and it's always necessary to deviate now and then, but on a typical day at 7pm it's Daddy & Mommy time. Good night, kiddos, we'll see you in the morning! It's healthy for their little bodies, my sanity, and our marriage. *If your kids don't have a consistent bedtime, what sort of nightly routine could you create to help them develop one?*

Work to maintain an efficient home.

Isn't it ironic that we have to work hard in order to rest well? But if the house is a wreck with no cleanclothes and no food for dinner, how *restful* will it really feel? I'm finding that the more I invest in the home, the more my family enjoys being in it. But there's a fine balance! As I'm doing my best to manage the home diligently, I must remember to...

Love the people in the home more than the tasks of the home.

Of all the items on my list, this is the hardest for me. Isn't that a *sad* confession? It is to me too. And yet the primary reason our home isn't more restful is because I can be a drill sergeant about maintaining it. Slowly, I'm beginning to realize that this is idolatry; it's loving "order" more than God's mandate to be kind and gracious with my family. *Is your approach to maintaining the home balanced? Do you need to become more diligent, or more gracious?*

Have a daily "down time" for the kids.

This can take a variety of different forms. Obviously, for babies and toddlers, nap time is their natural "down time." Since my preschoolers have outgrown naps, I break their quiet time into segments. They have a little alone time in their room, some sibling play time either outside or in the playroom, and some TV time. *Depending on the ages of your kids, how could you establish a designated "down time" for them every day?*

Find opportunities to bless your husband with alone time.

I know my husband often feels guilty taking time to himself. Because he works all day, he feels like every other moment should be spent with the kids. But if he's going to serve and lead our family well, he *needs* time to rest and rejuvenate. *What does your husband find restful? How can you provide rest for him this week?*

Be at peace with those within the home.

Nothing transforms a restful home into a war zone faster than discord. Colossians 3:12-17 urges believers to bear with one another, to forgive one another, to allow the peace of Christ to rule in our hearts, and to let the Word of God dwell so richly within us that we admonish one another in wisdom and gratitude. Let me ask you two last questions that I'm also asking myself: *Am I at peace with every member of my household? If not, what steps can I take today, to restore the peace?*

How Much Should a Mom Minister Outside the Home?

Tug of war. That's what comes to mind when I think of this question. On one end of the rope, I see this narcissistic, household-consumed version of myself who dreams about Pottery Barn bedding and pre-school drama to the neglect of all the people beyond the four walls of my home. On the other end of the rope, I see this frazzled, crazy version of myself delivering homemade casseroles to every sick family in church while my own kids eat microwavable corn dogs in front of the television.

How do we find balance? I always assumed I just needed to find the "middle of the rope." Which is a very vague way of saying, "Just try harder to be, well, *balanced*." If you could see my schedule now, I think it would look fairly balanced on the outside. I serve in two different ministries at church, which helped me say "No" to serving in a third ministry outside of church. We spend a few evenings a week with others, and a few at home by ourselves. But the truth is, this isn't really an outward question. It's not a logical, "what does your schedule look like?" kind of question. It's an emotional and spiritual question, often laden with guilt, presuppositions, and preferences. A heart question. And as we all know, our schedule can look ship-shape while our heart is in turmoil.

On Sunday night I dropped my kids off at our church nursery so I could serve at a youth event. It was a whiny, reluctant drop-off because *"What?! So-and-so-friend isn't here tonight?!"* Being the godly mom that I am, I promised them each a cupcake when the event was over, and said good-bye. As the youth band played I thought about...my kids. And my kids, and my kids, and my kids. "Oh God," I prayed, "I want to be *present* here tonight. I want to serve these students. Help me recognize that I'm called to more than just my family." And as His peace washed over me, a new thought occurred. Maybe ministering inside and outside the home aren't on two different ends of a rope. Maybe, in God's perfect design, they actually *work together* to make us better at both.

Think about it like this—how do we become the kind of women who have the character and wisdom to shepherd those outside our home? *By first being faithful inside our home.* A reader once referred me to an article in which a married blogger was reluctant to have children because she didn't want to shortchange her ministry. The blogger explained that when she got married, she felt like she took a "back seat" to her husband in ministry. The last thing she wanted was to have children and be rendered entirely invisible at their church. The blogger's conclusion was to abandon gender roles, whereby she and her husband could do all things interchangeably.

The reader who referred me to this article was understandably confused by it. "Is this the right perspective?" she asked me. In my opinion, no. It's not. I can say that with confidence because the Bible flips this perspective upside-down. In Titus 2:3-5, Paul instructs, "Teach the older women to be reverent in the way they live...Then they can train the younger women to love their husbands and children, to be self-controlled and pure, to be busy at home, to be kind, and to be subject to their husbands, so that no one will malign the word of God."

Obviously God is passionate about the home. So passionate, in fact, that one of the chief ways He wants women to minister to other women is by training them to be faithful in the home! How can we fulfill this mandate if we're never home *learning* these lessons ourselves? In this way, our home isn't an obstacle to ministry, it's a platform and training ground for it.

On the flip side, I also believe that as we embrace God's calling to serve those outside our home, we become *better* wives and mothers to those within the home! Consider this—what message are we sending our children if we're constantly consumed with them? More importantly, is it a biblical one? Growing up, my mom imparted many lessons to me without ever saying a word. As she counseled sobbing women on the sofa, I learned that she was more than just my mom, and that there were things that were more important than playing tea party with me *right now!* I learned that there was great suffering in the world, and one of the ways we could love Jesus was by loving others.

So how do we find balance? I think it begins with that popular word we all love so much: submission. If you resent the way your family limits your freedom in ministry, you need to submit to the biblical truth that God has called you to serve your family, trusting that as you obey Him, He will groom you to more effectively minister to others. If you idolize your family to the neglect of the rest of the body of Christ, you need to submit to the biblical truth that the best way to love your family is to make *Jesus* primary, trusting that in doing this, you will be a better wife and mom. Either way, the answer lies in submitting our own preferences and personal agendas to Christ.

These are some of the questions I've been stewing over as I check my own heart:

- *Do I regularly meet my husband and children's needs for love, attention, and affirmation? If they were honest, what would they say?*
- *Is the way that I manage our household a blessing or a burden to my family?*
- *Does it concern me when I hear that others are suffering? Does my prayer life reflect this concern? Do my actions?*
- *Am I open and sensitive to God leading me to serve others, or am I quick to assume "I've got my hands full"?*
- *Is there an area outside my home where I have felt burdened to serve God, but have not obeyed? Is there an area outside my home where my husband has challenged me to serve God, but I have been unwilling to even consider it?*
- *Has my husband, or a spiritual mentor, ever suggested I may be over-committed in ministry, to the detriment of my family or my own well-being?*
- *Why am I motivated to serve my family and others? Am I motivated by love for Christ, or love for myself?*

Clearly God has called us to *both* the home and those outside of it. That can only mean these two mandates are not at odds with one another, but rather, working together to make us the women he wants us to be. Forget tug of war. Instead, picture a bicycle with two pedals pumping in unison. One propels the other forward, and vice versa. It's the only way the bike can balance.

When Homemaking Becomes Idolatrous

Back when I was learning how to drive, my dad used to say, "You drive the car. Don't let the car drive you." He said it whenever I was going too fast and starting to lose control. I thought about that expression a lot last week. It was one of those up-all-night-with-vomiting-children kind of weeks. Toss home renovation chaos and 32 weeks of pregnancy into the mix, and I was left with a simple choice: either escape to a coffee shop the second my husband got home, or risk internal combustion.

"In other words," I explained to Clint one afternoon, "this cup of coffee, and more importantly the *silence* surrounding it, is a matter of life or death." He let me go.

The moment the scent of macchiato wafted through my hair, my mind started to clear. I thought about all that I was escaping: five loads of post-vomit laundry waiting to be folded, *endless* bickering over an Elsa doll I would've paid a thousand dollars to multiply into two, enough toys on the living room floor to start my own business, enough crumbs on the carpet to feed a village of mice...

"You manage the home. Don't let the home manage you." *Hmmm...* Suddenly, I was fifteen years old again, trying to drive a car that was completely out of control. It's so ironic that something as worthy as the calling to manage a home can become one of the greatest sources of idolatry and sin in my life. It's been this way for me for a long time now. I'm the kind of person who would prefer to clean my whole house, then race to pick up the kids from school looking like I just escaped from a refugee camp, rather than risk returning to a *home* that looks like a refugee camp. It's just my thing—the idol I am always drawn to. And you know what the truth is? It really has nothing to do with the house at all.

When everything is clean and orderly around me, I feel like my heart is clean and orderly. I feel like I'm in control. Like I'm successful. And *that* is what drives me. It's that God-like feeling (delusion really) that I can manage the messes in my heart by managing the messes in my home. But as all neat-freaks know, it's as fleeting as a clean countertop. And here's the *really* ironic part: all the time I'm parading around like a goddess in control of her universe, the house is actually controlling me. It's governing my emotions and reactions. Dictating my choices and attitudes. It's not my minion, it's my master. Why else would I feel the need to escape?

And it's not just limited to cleaning either. As I prepare to have another baby, my nesting instincts are on over-drive, staggering beneath a mountain of paint samples and Pottery Barn catalogues. Is it so bad that I want my whole house to look beautiful? To be a warm and inviting (and maybe slightly envy-evoking) place? *Ach, the balancing act!* I wish I could sort through the attitudes in my heart like I sort through the kids' toys: "Desire to bless my family with a beautiful home?" *Fantastic, we'll keep that.* "Egotistical drive to feel good about myself?" *Yuck, into the garbage.* "Longing to serve others? To enjoy and embrace my calling as a homemaker?" *Awesome!* "Competitive, materialistic spirit, consumed with earthly things?" *Trash!*

But the bad motivations in my heart aren't like the onions I can just pluck out of the kids' dinner. They're woven in deeply, like a virus. What I need is the antidote. I need the true answer for the aches and desires of my heart.

I need to remember that this longing to "nest" is really a longing for security and stability. It is my heart's cry for a place of belonging. And into this deep heartache, Jesus offers security, identity, and purpose. He looks at me (and you) and says, "You are a **chosen** people, a royal priesthood, a holy nation, a people **belonging** to God, that you may declare the praises of him who called you out of darkness into his wonderful light."[32] He looks at me (and you) scrubbing vomit out of the carpet at 2am and He says, "**My grace** is sufficient for you, for my **power** is made perfect in weakness."[33] He looks at me (and you) racing through dishes and diapers, carpools and catalogues, trying our very best to just be *good enough,* and He says, "You have been crucified with Me, and you no longer live, but I live in you. So live this life on earth by **faith** in Me, because I love you and I gave myself up for you."[34]

Security, identity, purpose. Hope, strength, grace. How foolish to believe we could find these things in a can of paint or an organized playroom! Does this mean we toss in the towel and go ahead and register for a guest appearance on *Hoarders: Buried Alive?* No...tempting as that may sound. Hebrews 12:1 says you and I have been called to a race. It started the moment we surrendered to Christ, and it will end the day we cross the finish line and land in His arms. We must keep running, but just as importantly, we must ask ourselves *why* we are running. Are we running to be accepted, or are we running because we already are? Are we running for the heavenly prize, or an earthly one? Oh how tragic it would be to cross the finish line with a gorgeous home and a lifetime of aimless running.[35]

Woman

"THE FACT THAT I AM A WOMAN DOES NOT MAKE ME A DIFFERENT KIND OF CHRISTIAN, BUT THE FACT THAT I AM A CHRISTIAN MAKES ME A DIFFERENT KIND OF WOMAN."

Elisabeth Elliot

Guilt-Free Womanhood

Wake up running, try your best,
No time today to take a rest,
The dishes weren't done before bed last night,
And now the kitchen's a miserable sight.

"Sit in your chair, don't argue with me,
I've got lots to do, can't you see?"
Hurry, rush, clean, clean, clean,
I wonder if my tone was mean?

It's grocery day, no time to lose,
Button their coats, slip on their shoes.
Gee, these hand-me-downs look rough,
**Sigh! I never dress them well enough!*

In the store a thousand choices,
In my head a thousand voices:
"You shouldn't be paying so much for that,
You shouldn't be buying those salty snacks..."

On and on, the voices come,
Talking 'til the day is done.
Wash the dishes, sweep the floor,
Work 'til there is nothing more.

Then lay in bed, my spirits sagging,
Count the ways I've come up lacking:
Forgot to make my husband's lunch,
Processed snacks for the kids to munch,

Should have served my husband more,
Shouldn't have skipped that extra chore.
Gave in to the chocolate crave,
Growing a new species in the microwave!

Did my kids see the gospel today?
Did we spend enough time in play?
Oh, how come womanhood seems to be
Synonymous with "guilt" for me?

I wonder what the Lord would say,
If I let Him speak into my day?
Perhaps He'd take me by the hand,
And lead me to His Word again.

To a place where Mary was rewarded
For leaving her tasks in order to worship.
To a well where a guilty woman like me,
Drank of the Water that set her free.

And to a city where a whore's red rope,
Bought for her a living Hope.
Maybe He'd take me back in time,
To the woman who pushed ahead in line,

Just to touch the tip of His cloak,
Believing it would rid her an awful yoke.
Or to the woman at the foot of a Cross,
Weeping for the Son she'd lost.

All of these women knew in their being
That He is the greatest reason for living.
And so in the midst of their crazy lives,
They didn't hold up "effort" and expect a prize.

Instead they hurled all pretense aside,
And ran for the Arms spread open wide!
And with their pride tossed to the wind,
They staked all hope on ***belonging*** *to Him.*

Tomorrow, start over, and wake up smiling,
Sing for the joy of simply belonging,
Live by His power like the woman of old
Who touched His robe with faith so bold.

Claim the truth, when you feel guilty,
Like the Samaritan—believe you are free!
Remember the faith that Rahab had,
Then sing of His mercy, rejoice, and be glad!

Hold to the Cross in smooth winds and rough,
Don't live like His death wasn't enough.
And if you should find yourself suddenly flailing,
Be then like Mary, and choose ye the better thing.[36]

The Woman I Wish I Could Be

Do you ever feel like there's a gigantic gap between the woman you are and the one you want to be? I do. The woman I want to be lives in my mind, somewhere between the endless to-do lists and the names of all the Sesame Street Muppets. She is innately patient. Fearlessly radical. She believes that God is faithful, even when it feels like He's forgotten her. She always chooses the better thing—to feed her soul instead of her flesh, to submit instead of defy, to rejoice instead of complain. She never snaps at her children or nags her husband.

In fact, the only person she ever irritates is me. She eludes me and haunts me at the same time. She is the woman I think about five seconds after I say the thing I shouldn't have said. The woman I think about when my kids are in bed and I'm wishing I hadn't been so impatient with them. I think about her when I meet someone really sunny who never seems to doubt God. And I think about her on the really cloudy days when I feel guilty for not climbing out of my own discouragement.

I used to think I could bridge the gap between her and me in one giant leap. Maybe attend a Beth Moore conference? A weekend prayer retreat? But I never could make the leap. At times I thought I had, and then inevitably I would disappoint myself. Struggle with the same old sin. Fail in the same old way.

Sometime this summer it finally clicked with me. The journey from me to her is a *small step* journey. It is not made up of grandiose conferences or life-altering experiences. It is made up of millions upon millions of *tiny moments.* Paul David Tripp taught me this when he wrote:

> ...the character and quality of our life is forged in little moments. We tend to back away from the significance of these little moments because they *are* little moments. [But] these are the moments that make up our lives.[37]

In context, he was writing about all the little thoughts, words, and choices that shape a marriage and set the stage for the future. But I am finding this "small-moment approach" is a great way to live *all* of life. I have come to pray a very simple prayer throughout the day. Whether I'm believing a lie, battling idols, or itching to erupt, in the heat of the moment all I pray is, "God, help me win this small-moment battle!" That's all I focus on. I don't think about overcoming every battle, or making a personal sanctification plan, or donning a cape and painting Supermom across my forehead. I just focus on the one small battle before me, and by God's power with Christ's help, I fight to win. Then, ten minutes later, when the baby dumps a bowl of spaghetti onto my mother-in-law's carpet, I pray, "God, help me win this small-moment battle!" And so it goes.

You build a house one brick at a time, write a book one word at a time, and live a life one moment at a time. You and I don't have to become the Proverbs 31 woman tomorrow. We just have to throw ourselves upon the grace and power of Christ to live faithfully *today.* To make the wise choice. To say the kind thing. To reject the awful thought. To repent and get back up again. And one day we will look back and realize that over a lifetime—over a million small moments—*God grew us.*

Mother Theresa, Adolf Hitler, Martin Luther, Jessica Simpson—they all have one thing in common. They became who they are one small moment at a time. And so will we.

Dangerous Daydreams

For as long as I can remember, "imagination" has had a good rep. And I have had a generous supply of it. As a kid I didn't just "wrap Christmas presents;" I performed surgery on anxious patients with nothing but pink safety scissors and a roll of Scotch tape. I didn't "iron clothes" for my mother; I hosted a televised special on how to get wrinkles out of an Oxford. Imagination, I quickly learned, was a great way to pass the time. And the sorrow.

If I didn't make the team, I imagined I was the star player. If the cute boy didn't like me, I imagined that he did. And if the cute boy turned out to be a real jerk, well that was the beauty of imagination! In five seconds flat I could turn him into the man of my dreams. I always assumed I'd quit daydreaming once some of these dreams were actually realized. After all, when I had the amazing job, and the exciting life, and the man of my dreams I wouldn't need to daydream, right?

Unless I didn't have those things. Unless somewhere along the way I had created dreams so lofty no reality could compete with them. No man fulfill them. No set of circumstances live up to them. I was probably in my twenties when I finally realized daydreaming could be dangerous. That it could pave a fast track to discontentment.

I think a lot about it now as I raise young girls—girls who have already fallen in love with the notion of princesses and fairytales. On the one hand, I'm a major advocate for imagination. Give me an empty car and a long road trip, and I'll give Walter Mitty a run for his money. But as a woman who's a smidgen wiser than I used to be, I sidle up to it warily. Imagine we're in a fort cooking dinner out of pine cones? I'm all about it! Imagine we're digging for dinosaur bones? Let's do it! Imagine one day every fairy tale wish will come true and life will be perfect? *Don't do it.* Oh, my sweet little girls, *don't do it.*

Because the truth is, you and I were never made for the fairytale. We weren't made to live comfortable, easy lives that always make us feel good. We were made to live one real life, with a real God, who offers real hope, in a real and broken world.

Shortly before leaving His disciples, Jesus warned them that suffering was coming. He said He was preparing them for it so that in HIM they may have peace. And then He made this promise: "In this world, you will have trouble. But take heart! **I** have overcome the world."[38]

The answer to the reality of pain, the reason we can stand up under it, has and always will be found in Jesus. That's the mistake I made so many years ago when I didn't make the team and the cute boy didn't like me. *I didn't run to Jesus* to remind myself that my worth is securely kept in Him. I didn't let Jesus satisfy my longing to be known and loved. Instead I crafted a really puny version of fulfillment and daydreamed about it. And as soon as the daydream was over, so was the satisfaction.

How much wiser it would be to embrace reality, and more importantly, to embrace the God who enables us to endure it.

To Those Battling Biblical Womanhood

Recently someone asked me to respond to an article bashing biblical womanhood. Admittedly, it's one subject where I've been fairly silent. Partly for fear of the backlash. But mostly because I am the last person who deserves to write about it. It's not that I ever rejected God's call to submit to my husband and to have the sort of spirit that's beautiful in God's sight.[39] In fact, I embraced such teaching as sound doctrine from a wise and sovereign God. The problem was I couldn't *live* it to save my life.

As a kid I was fairly compliant. So naturally, when I walked down the aisle, I believed this whole biblical womanhood thing would come easily for me. Sweet and submissive as a baby bunny. Boy, was my husband lucky! Then somewhere within our first year of marriage, Xena Warrior Princess rose up within me and slaughtered the bunny. What I once believed to be compliance, I now recognize was pride. Back then it manifested itself in the arrogant belief that I could fulfill the call to biblical womanhood in my own strength. Once I realized I couldn't, it manifested itself in utter outrage that I should ever be asked to. *Why should I submit? I'm smart and gifted. I can get it done twice as well in half the time.* And so I became controlling, disrespectful, and angry. But I could never control things as completely as I wanted to, which only made me more furious. Finally, all the anger gave way to deep discontentment.

Maybe you can relate. Maybe you can't. Maybe the entire notion of biblical womanhood makes you want to gag. Here is my challenge. If the thought of submitting to an honorable man feels old-fashioned or degrading to you, then for just a moment, set it aside. Forget all about submission and respect as it relates to a man, and ask yourself the one question I was forced to confront: *Am I willing to submit to God?*

I finally came to see that my real fight was with Him. It wasn't my husband's role I wanted; it was God's. I longed for the authority to control my life as I saw fit. Like Satan himself, my heart cried, "I will make myself like the Most High."[40] I'll never forget the day God opened my eyes to what I was becoming. As I cried on my knees, He gave me a new verse from Isaiah 26:3: "You will keep in perfect peace him whose mind is steadfast, because he trusts in you." Oh how I longed for peace! And I saw that it only came by way of trust. Deep down, if I really *trusted* God, I could stop trying to *be* Him. Then instead of being thrown into turmoil by the things I couldn't control, my mind would be steadfast. And all the anger, anxiety, and discord I'd welcomed into my heart and home would be replaced, at last, with peace.

We often view submission as oppressive, but I'll tell you, that day as I submitted to God, I'd never felt more free in my life. The truth is, biblical submission has and always will be foundational to Christianity. To quote Merrian-Webster, to submit is "to yield oneself to the authority or will of another."[41] Is this not the very heart and soul of the gospel? Indeed this is the example Christ Himself set when He submitted to the Father's will, becoming obedient to the point of death.[42] And that is exactly what's required of any who would follow Him. The call to Christianity is not a call to rule, but to die. To become a bondservant; a slave to the One True King, and in so doing, to discover life and freedom for the very first time.[43]

Do I believe God has a distinct vision for womanhood? Yes, I do. If He wanted men and women to function in exactly the same way, I believe He could've made one gender. We could've reproduced asexually, like star fish. *But He didn't.* He could've made Eve first. Or inspired Paul to urge men to be keepers of the home, subject to their wives. *But He didn't.* He intentionally created both men and women, and through Scripture revealed the equal but different roles for which He designed them.

If you struggle with the doctrine or application of biblical womanhood, would you be willing to begin by yielding to the authority of Christ, then asking Him to teach you *His* vision for womanhood, as revealed in the Bible? Not what you *want* the Bible to teach, or think the Bible *should* teach, but what it actually teaches. Because as Wayne Grudem points out, when we tweak Scripture to suit our preferences, what's ultimately at stake isn't merely manhood or womanhood. It's the authority of the Bible itself.[44]

Innocent Envy

Come along,
Won't you come with me,
Down an innocent trail.
Feast your eyes
On another man's life,
'Til all in your world grows pale.
Measure his days,
Number his gifts,
Weigh them against your own.
And if you should find
A life more sublime,
Then bitterly curse and moan.
But if by a chance,
Your innocent glance,
Does prove you better than he,
Then lift up your hands!
Triumphantly dance,
For the god you surely must be.

Come along,
Won't you come with me,
You're hungry and thirsty for more.
What about him?
Can you possibly win,
And lengthen your pitiful score?
You cannot, you mourn,
His life is adorned
With blessing and beauty galore!
You know who's to blame?
I'll whisper his name,
The GOD who's failed you once more.
Wave your fist high!
Bellow and cry,
For my words, I promise, are true:
The God who unjustly
Blessed him so richly,
Certainly cares not for you.

Come along,
Won't you come with me,
I can make it all right.
You need just another,
Unlucky brother,
To restore your superior height.
Look all around,
Fume now and frown,
Measure and weigh and judge,
The rules of the game
Are always the same,
And the chains, they never do budge.

Come along,
Won't you come with me,
The view is practically free...
Just for a start,
Lend me your heart,
And all that you hope to be.

Why Women Wander

From the time we're young society feeds us a steady diet of lies: find the right man and you'll be satisfied, attain the right figure and you'll be beautiful, wear the right clothes and you'll be accepted. So we try it, only to discover there's still this quiet ache.

Like a boat without an anchor, our hearts drift restlessly on a constant quest for fulfillment. And boy does the world have a lot of suggestions for where we might find fulfillment. I'm not much of a magazine reader, but I recently picked up a magazine promising to divulge how Jennifer Hudson "lives it up at Christmas without putting on a pound." Inadvertently, I stumbled upon an article entitled "12 Things We Learned about Love in 2012."[45] The list was nothing short of devastating, boosting the pornographic novel *Fifty Shades of Grey* and the male-strip-club movie *Magic Mike. Really?* These are the things we learned about *love?* But the sad reality is *yes,* these are the tutors shaping the hearts and minds of countless women.

And it's all counterfeit. We desire intimacy, and we're offered lust. We long for significance, and we're handed a J Crew catalogue. We want a Hero, and the world suggests Channing Tatum in his underwear. Speaking of heroes, the other night I watched *The Bourne Legacy* with my husband. One particular scene had me especially hooked. In it the female doctor is running from the police. She escapes into a narrow alley, only to find a police officer on either side. Meanwhile, her partner, the medically enhanced super-duper spy is also running from police on the rooftops. Just as you think it's all over for the doctor, her partner leaps from a roof, flies down this tight alley, and saves her. Ridiculous, sure, but I loved it! I always love that image of the mighty hero rescuing the girl. I think a lot of women do. You know why I think it appeals to us? Because it's a dim reflection of a true story.

The morning after watching the movie, we were singing at church when a line from the song struck me: *"The King of Glory rescued me."* Unbidden, the image from the movie flashed through my mind. With it came the joyous thought—there really *is* a Hero! The world may offer an array of counterfeits, but there is a *real thing* in existence. There is a Hero who longs to be deeply intimate with you, who has the power to bestow true significance, and who makes the Hulk look like a girl scout. He is the ultimate leader, stronger than any super-spy, and fiercer than any warrior.

If you want to see His heroism in action, just stop by Psalm 18 and listen to what God does when David cries out for help. With fire from His mouth and anger that makes the mountains tremble, God flies swiftly on the wings of the wind, His voice thundering like hailstones. He battles with arrows and lightning, until the channels of the sea are seen and the foundations of the world laid bare at His rebuke. And then David declares, "He sent from on high, He took me; He drew me out of many waters. He rescued me from my strong enemy…for they were too mighty for me."[46] Talk about a rescue! Talk about a *Hero.*

Why do women wander? Because our souls were made for this Hero, and nothing less can satisfy. As a Christian, do I still feel the temptation to wander aimlessly? Absolutely. It's why I'm writing. But I take heart because I also know the truth. That restless stirring in my heart is not the need for a new pair of skinny jeans, or a few more dates with my husband. It is my soul's soft reminder that I was made for Christ. It is my Savior's invitation to come and be satisfied.

What I Want My Daughters to Know about Biblical Womanhood

My dear daughters,

Being a godly woman begins with surrendering your whole heart to Jesus. This means Jesus defines who you are—not your friends, the world, or even yourself. The Bible says that those who surrender their hearts to Jesus are blessed, chosen, holy, adopted, loved, and forgiven.[47] My precious daughters, no matter how you feel, or what happens to you, that is your identity. Surrendering your heart to Jesus also means obeying Him. Often (just like your mom) you will be tempted to be the boss of your life, following your own wisdom. But the Bible says "the foolishness of God is wiser than men, and the weakness of God is stronger than men."[48] If you build your life around Jesus, submitting to the perfect wisdom of God, He will make you the woman He wants you to be, which is the true definition of biblical womanhood.

As you grow, you will learn that the world tries to define womanhood by outward actions and appearances. Many people believe beauty is the ultimate goal of womanhood. Our culture will tempt you to believe that the prettier and sexier you are, the more valuable and loved you will be. But this is a lie! I Peter

3:3-4 says that our main focus should not be looking pretty on the outside, but rather having a gentle and quiet spirit, which is very precious to God. Do you know what a gentle and quiet spirit is? The word "quiet" doesn't mean you can't be loud and bubbly (which your daddy and I find absolutely adorable.) It means your *heart* is as quiet and peaceful as a baby resting with its mother.[49] You see, when you listen to Jesus' opinion of you, you will not be anxious about fitting in or being the most beautiful. Your heart will be at peace. And *that* is true beauty.

Some people believe finding the right man is the ultimate goal of womanhood. But this will always lead to disappointment! If God wants you to be single, you may believe the lie that you're less adequate than wives and moms. If He wants you to marry, you may believe the lie that a man can provide lasting fulfillment. My sweet girls, stand guard against both thoughts! God has always based biblical womanhood, first and foremost on our relationship with Him, not men. If He does bless you with a godly husband, then respect, cherish, and honor that man, for he is a gift! But do not look to him for your ultimate hope and security. That is Jesus' specialty alone.

Finally, my dear girls, beware of defining biblical womanhood by what you do. If you fall into this trap, you will forever be comparing yourself with others—how well you cook, clean, decorate, and discipline; whether or not you stay at home; how you invest your time and talents. This can only lead to pride, shame, guilt, and judgment. Always remember, biblical womanhood is about *attitudes* more than actions. It is about having a soft and submissive heart toward God and His commands. Most of God's instructions in the Bible apply to both men and women. But there are certain passages written specifically for women.[50] Embrace the teaching of these passages with a grateful heart! They were not written to burden you with guilt, but to teach you God's perfect will and design for women. He alone can, and will, empower you to be the woman He wants you to be. And in becoming what *He* wants, you will find the greatest freedom and joy.

All my love forever,
Mom

Here's to the Woman Inside the Mom

I love writing for many honorable reasons. But I also love it for one selfish reason. It's something that's mine. *All mine.* I never realized what a commodity that could be until I became a mom. In the beginning, I was only asked to give up little things: time, sleep, my waistline. And then they started crawling and I surrendered a little more: tidiness, order, all of the keys on my laptop (which FYI, can actually be popped right off.) Then one day I blinked and there they were—chattering away a mile a minute, going to pre-school, making friends, getting their feelings hurt, asking big questions, challenging my authority, drawing me pictures, jumping in bed to kiss my very pregnant belly and perhaps ride it like a cowgirl... And I realized there wasn't a square inch of my personhood they hadn't entirely and eternally invaded.

I love them with these dry, un-manicured hands that wash their dishes and scrub their faces and brush their hair and tie their shoes. I love them with these swollen ankles that race around town taking them places. I love them with this horrifyingly out-of-tune voice that sings them to sleep, and lays down the law, and tells them stories about when I was a little girl. I love them with this face that will probably wrinkle up like a prune by the time I'm 45 because it's so used to smooching small cheeks and making silly faces. I love them with the eyes that always know where they are, the ears that hear their cries even when Daddy is snoring, and the mind that remembers Tuesday is Johnny Appleseed day and we must wear red to school. I love them with the soul that begs God for their salvation, and I love them with the heart I have lifted out of my chest and tucked away in theirs.

Truly, I love this lot of mine. And yet, at the very same time, there are days when I go to a coffee shop and see college girls writing papers and giggling about boys, and I remember what it was like to have a mind that was completely my own. To be consumed with nobody else's problems. To think about nobody else's needs. To dream dreams just for me, and pursue ambitions just because I could. I remember what it was like to have things that were *mine*.

When I write I enter a tiny corner of the world that's all mine. It's the place where I remember that there's more to me than grocery lists and Windex spray. And for one or two hours when I sit down at the computer, I don't think about the crusty broccoli under the table or the mismatched socks in the hamper. Instead of looking outward, I look inward. I think about the *woman* who picks up the broccoli and sorts through the socks. I think about how *she* feels, what *she* needs, who *she* is. It would be so easy for me to lose her. In the mayhem of everyday life, it would be easy to go through the motions and then collapse in front of the TV. To grow completely out of touch with the woman inside the mom. To shush her, ignore her, numb her... until one day she bursts into tears at the dinner table and everybody wonders why.

That's one of the reasons I write. Because I need to stay in touch with that woman. I need to know how she's doing. I need to speak the gospel over her heart and life. Otherwise, she won't make it. Sure, she'll still flip pancakes and drive carpools, but underneath it all her heart will grow hard and her spirit cynical.

With all that being said, there are times when this little world of mine needs to grow quiet. Times when fevers and holidays and back-to-school jitters require my full attention. And in those seasons, I'll have you know, I miss you. I miss the way the woman inside of this mom gets to connect with the woman inside of you. But believe me, no matter the season, whether I get to write or not, I will still slip away to check up on the woman underneath the nursing tops and smudged mascara. I will find moments to speak gospel truth over her. And I hope you will too. I hope that in the midst of your busy days, you will find quiet moments to slip away and spend time with the woman inside of you, and with the God who loves her so very much.

Child

"But courage, child: we are all between the paws of the true Aslan."

C.S. Lewis, *The Last Battle*

The Master's {Violent} Mercy

I had a dream that long I sat
Upon a distant shore,
And trembled lonely in the storm,
And knew myself no more.

There was a Voice to steady me,
But I lost it in the wind.
And so I knew not who I was,
Nor who I'd ever been.

I listened to the roaring waves,
And to the sand and sea,
I let them tell me how to think,
And who I was to be.

Until I feared the sea would rise
And crush me with its spite,
And drown my hope upon the rocks,
And snuff the day to night.

I called to the Master of the Sea;
I knew that He could save.
For once upon a distant time,
He spoke to the wind and waves.

But He would not calm the raging storm,
He only held my hand,
And let it beat us bruised and bloody,
Over the calloused sand.

I fought and groaned and cursed aloud,
I wept into His face.
I judged Him for His cruelty,
I blamed His failing grace.

Then He lifted me into His arms,
And whispered, "Do not mourn.
This is not where mercy dies,
But the place that it is born.

I have not come to spare you the storm
That threatens peace and health,
But to use the very storm you fear,
To save you from yourself."

It was then I knew His endless grace,
Had come to change within,
And at the very end of me,
At last we could begin.

The Things in My Life I Don't Like

A godly mentor once told me that joy and sorrow are like two sides to a railroad track. Both run through our lives in surprisingly close proximity. At the time I didn't really get it. I believed the angst of college life would subside around the time I put on a pair of strappy black heels and received a diploma. And it did. Good-bye final exams, good riddance college drama. But sure as the dawn, new sorrows came. Indeed, every season seems to have its share. Some are gigantic, others minor. But always, there is *something.* Something I want. Something I fear. Something that exhausts me. Something that confuses me. Something that disappoints me. In my life, I can *always* find something to complain about. I can always find a reason to be discontent. A reason to question God.

The ironic thing is, at the very same time there's a track of joy running through my life. For every handful of cheerios shoved into the heating vents(*ugh!*) there's one little cheerio poked into a bellybutton that sets off a symphony of laughter. And for every private struggle with God, there is the promise of deeper intimacy, truer understanding, and richer communion. I think the secret to contentment lies in learning how to embrace both sides of the railroad track—the things in our lives we love, and the things in our lives we don't. How do we do that? I think it begins by…

Being Honest

Contrary to social media myth, nobody enjoys *everything* about his or her life, because no life is untouched by the fall. The question is: Are we being honest about the painful side of the track? Few things are more freeing than authenticity. And no people are freer to embrace authenticity than Christians *because we have guaranteed acceptance.* We are not judged according to how well we "have it all together," how we perform, or how many people we can deceive into envying us. We live in the shadow of another Man's perfection which forever declares us righteous, accepted, and loved! So we're free to risk, to fail, to be rejected by the world, to be struggling, growing, and honest about it.

Conversely, nothing is more enslaving than deceit. When we can't be real with anybody, including ourselves, we live in a narrow prison of appearances. What's more, honesty with God is paramount to a relationship with Him. Lying to yourself is denial. Lying to others is pretense. But lying to God is the very depths of loneliness.

Being Humble

Once we're honest about the trials in our life, and we quit pretending we're not as disappointed as we really are, we can begin to view them through a lens of humility. Like the spoonful of sugar that helps the medicine go down, humility can make the toughest trial easier to swallow, simply by putting it into *perspective.*

What this means is, it's time to take your eyes off your belly button, and look up into the face of Christ. There is no quicker, truer way to cultivate humility. Believe me; nobody is more navel-focused than me. Just the other night I had a conversation with friends about how annoyingly introspective I am. Because of this, the "honesty" part is not really my struggle. The humility part is. Yet time and again humility proves to be my ticket to peace with suffering. For in light of Christ, my sorrows are pale, my indignation arrogant, and my "rights" ridiculous.

Being Hopeful

So picture you and me—shamefully honest, pitifully humble, a bundle of unworthiness in His presence. Pretty pathetic, huh? Wouldn't you know, our gracious God looks at us, and unlike the world, He does not despise us. As He said to Israel in the depth of her disgrace, *"How can I give you up…My heart is turned over within Me, All My compassions are kindled."*[51]

In our honest, naked humility, Jesus Christ imparts hope. He has not left us. He has not ceased to love us. He is greater. Stronger. And in *Him* lies the victory. Often my disappointment with the painful track in my life is intertwined with discouragement over my own sinfulness. *I shouldn't have these feelings of anxiety, disappointment, or anger. I should be past this. Better than this. More mature in Christ than this.* But there is a truth that continually sustains me. It is the mystery of Colossians 1:27, "*Christ in (me), the hope of glory!*" Because Christ dwells in me, I always have hope. In Him I will overcome both my circumstances and my sinfulness, and one day, by His grace, *I will arrive.*

If you are in Christ, so will you. There will come a day when the mighty engine of Hope that's powered us along the tracks of joy and pain will deposit us in a place that knows no sorrow. On that day, there will be but one track stretching into eternity—that of joy fulfilled, faith seen, and hope realized.

On Leaving a Legacy

I ate an energy bar tonight thinking it was a granola bar, and two hours later I'm still wide awake. The house is unusually quiet, and for some reason my mind has drifted back to an old friend, one I find myself thinking about often.

When I was in Bible College there was this unbelievably beautiful girl in my education classes who one day slid her lunch tray beside mine and struck up a conversation. You know the kind of friend who grows on you slowly? Aimee wasn't like that. She was more like a diamond you find at a gas station—an extraordinary treasure in a completely ordinary world. She spoke fluent Mandarin, had dreams the size of Antarctica, zero pretenses, and a heart as genuinely alive as her bright blue eyes. That day we talked and laughed at the lunch table until every last scrap was cleared up and put away. And from then on, I loved Aimee Powell.

We would go out to eat, order something loaded with carbs and talk about all the things college girls love to talk about: classes, and boys, and friends, and Jesus, and all we hoped to do and be. I saw her giddy, and I saw her heartbroken. And I never once doubted that Aimee would lead a very grand life.

Then three years after graduating from college, on a boring January morning, Aimee was killed in a car accident. And just like that, in two seconds flat, I learned that she was gone. You want to know the truth? Part of me still can't believe it. Three years later I still cry when I think about her. I cry for myself because I miss her. I cry for the future I imagined she would have. I cry for her family because I know that if in four years she brought such joy to my life, she must've been sunshine in theirs.

But amid all the tears, I have a profound sense of peace when I think of Aimee. On the one hand, it seems maddeningly unfair. She never got to marry the dashingly handsome man I just knew she was destined for, never got to raise a house full of children or become famous and change the world. But as I watched the newscast about the accident, I listened to an anchor woman who didn't even know Aimee testify about Aimee's life—the students who loved her, the mission trips she took, the Facebook page that shared her passionate love for Jesus. And like lightning it struck me, *Aimee did it.* She ran the race all the way to the very end, and she crossed the finish line, *faithful.*

She didn't lead the extraordinary life I always imagined she would lead. Instead she led one ordinary life, with extraordinary faithfulness.

You know what? I think *that* is more inspiring than marrying a dashingly handsome man and changing the world.

Tonight I am proud of my friend. I am grateful to have been part of her beautiful life. And I am encouraged to follow her example and live this one, ordinary life of mine with all the extraordinary faithfulness only Jesus can supply, so that one day I, too, will cross the finish line victorious. This one's for you, my beautiful friend. Wish you were here with me tonight.

3 Things to Tell Yourself When Others Prosper While You Suffer

Have you ever noticed that suffering makes us keenly aware of the blessings of others? It's the woman recovering from a miscarriage who's the first to notice all the pregnant bellies in the grocery store. The laid-off employee who feels like every friend is celebrating a fulfilling career. The spread-thin single mom who watches husbands hauling baby carriers into church.

There was a season in my life when it felt like God said, "No," to every request I asked of Him. I stored up those "No's" in my heart like an old woman in a house full of cats, daily nursing my grievances with God. Finally, out of nowhere, I received an unexpected blessing. It was a very small thing, so when it fell through a few months later, my husband couldn't understand why I took it so hard. As we cooked in the kitchen (well, technically he was cooking and I was sobbing on a stool), I finally managed to choke, "It just felt like it was a *sign* that God still loved me."

In the weeks to come, God impressed three truths upon me that deeply comforted me and radically changed my perspective. The first was this:

I do not need a single blessing from God to know that He loves me. I only need to look to the cross to know that He loves me.

When we look solely at the circumstances of our lives, it often feels like God plays favorites. Like He loves sweet Susie Jane with her happy family and easy life more than He loves you and me. I used to comfort myself by thinking that one day the boot may drop on Susie Jane's perfect life too. But it may not. People really do face varying degrees of suffering while on earth. And even if the boot did squash Susie Jane for a season, is it really biblical to delight in her suffering? To hope for it, even? Of course not.

I still remember the day God whispered those words above into my heart. All at once I saw the cross again. And just like that, I had *proof*...MIGHTY proof that God had not forgotten me. Just like that, I didn't need to test Him anymore, because the test had been given on a hill long ago, and He had passed with flying colors. Months later, my insecurity was triggered all over again when a sweet friend received the very blessing I ached for. As I cried to God in bed, I could almost hear Him pleading with such earnest passion, *"Look to the cross! I promise I love you—look to the cross!"* You know what? In a thousand years I wouldn't trade that intimate and powerful moment for a fleeting, earthly blessing. This brings me to lesson #2:

In God's economy, spiritual blessing always outweighs earthly blessing.

In the allegorical book, *Hinds Feet on High Places,* Much-Afraid embarks on a journey to the High Places. As she is about to set off, the Shepherd promises her, "I have most carefully chosen for you two of the very best and strongest guides."[52] Much-Afraid is horrified to learn that the guides are named Suffering and Sorrow. But later in her journey, when the Shepherd asks her how she feels about them, this is what she says:

> I never could have believed it possible, Shepherd, but in a way I have come to love them...They do truly want to get me up to the High Places, not just because it is the commandment which You have given them, but also because they want a horrid coward like myself to get there and be changed. You know, Shepherd, it makes a great difference in my feelings towards them not to look upon them any longer with dread, but as friends who want to help me.[53]

This is exactly what passages like James 1:2-4 teach. *God designs suffering to make us more like Christ.* Much as I despise encountering Sorrow and Suffering on my own journey, they are the most excellent tutors I have ever known. And nothing is more encouraging than looking back over my life and realizing that because of them, I am no longer the cowardly girl I once was...or the arrogant teenager...or the idolatrous young adult. *That* is the truest blessing. *Becoming like Jesus* is more valuable than birthing children, or winning awards, or finding a spouse, or any other earthly blessing we could ever beg for.

I AM NOT CALLED TO EVALUATE THE LIVES AND CIRCUMSTANCES OF OTHERS...I AM ONLY CALLED TO FOLLOW GOD.

The final stop on my journey to accepting personal suffering in light of other people's prosperity was John 21:18-22. Right after Jesus prophesies about Peter's future death, Peter glances at John and says exactly what I would've said: "Lord, what about this man?" To which

Jesus beautifully replies, "If it is my will that he remain (alive) until I come, what is that to you? You follow me!"

Wow. And *ouch.* If it is My will, that *she* receive the blessing you wanted, what is that to you? If it is My will to write the story of your life completely differently than you wanted Me to, what is that to you? If it is My will to say "Yes" to *him* and "No" to you, what is that to you? *You follow me.*

Dear believer, you and I are called to one thing only. Jesus Himself. To love Him enough to follow Him...*no matter what.* As Much-Afraid finally came to see in the Valley of Loss:

> Right down in the depths of her own heart she really had but one passionate desire, not for the things which the Shepherd had promised, but for Himself. All she wanted was to be allowed to follow Him forever.[54]

Sometimes only valleys and deserts can teach us that.

If Only Everyone Could Just Like Me

True confession #879: I long for the approval of people. I mean *long* for it. There was a season in my life when I felt the anxiety over people's approval so acutely that I called my mom one night and told her, "Every night I go to bed and the last thing I think before falling asleep is that I hope I don't wake up in the morning." As usual, my mom surprised me. Rather than panicking (which I thought would've been entirely appropriate), she challenged me. "I don't believe you don't want to live another day, Jeanne. You just don't want to live another day *in this bondage.*" And just like that, I felt the first rays of hope. Because I realized it was true. I *did* want to live; I just didn't want to live *like this.*

Living in the idolatry of man's approval is like living on a weathervane. You swing here and there, back and forth, your emotions as unpredictable as the wind. Then one day you realize that in all this time you've gotten nowhere. You've just been spinning in circles. *Everybody loves me! Everybody hates me. I'm brilliant! I'm foolish. I'm wanted! I'm rejected.* It's always the same song, sung over and over in a thousand different scenarios. And the star of the song is always the same. *Me.*

I used to view the idol of approval as "people-worship." I was worshipping other people's thoughts and opinions. But the truth is, I'm not just concerned with their thoughts and opinions; I'm concerned with their thoughts and opinions *about me.* Which means the idol of approval isn't really about people-worship but self-worship. The person I'm bowing down to is me. The person who consumes my thoughts is me. The person holding me captive is me.

So maybe it's time I started singing a different song. Here's one that's been humming through my mind all morning:

Turn your eyes upon Jesus,
Look full in His wonderful face!
And the things of earth will grow strangely dim,
In the light of His glory and grace.

Do you believe it? Do you believe that Jesus is so radiant that when we fix our eyes on Him, the things of earth—all those circumstances in which we're so concerned with our own dignity—will grow strangely dim? Do you believe HE can *outshine* you? Outshine your problems? Your reputation? Your insecurity?

I do. I do because I've experienced it. Turning your eyes upon Jesus is like jumping off the weathervane and dancing in the rain. It's refreshing and cleansing and liberating. Not only does Jesus Christ define my worth, He calls me to Himself, reminding me that the story is so much bigger than whether or not so-and-so likes me.[55] The story is as BIG as His love, as AGONIZING as a bloody cross, as POWERFUL as an empty tomb and as URGENT as a coming King. Surely that is reason for you and I to take our eyes off our bellybuttons, and together with the Psalmist David, declare, "My eyes are ever toward the Lord."[56]

When All You Can Do Is Wait

I've never met anyone who loved waiting rooms. Think about it, nobody schedules a doctor's appointment to read the AARP magazines in the waiting room. You don't call Cox Cable to listen to the hold music, and you don't go to a restaurant for the fun of clutching a buzzer in your hand. Embracing the concept of waiting defies our sense of logic. Waiting is what we put up with to reach the goal. We endure it. Deal with it. Grumble our way through it. But we certainly don't embrace it. In many ways, waiting is the enemy. It is the hairline crack in our perfect plans that terrifies us, secretly makes us question if we're deficient. If God's deficient.

I use to view waiting as something akin to being a bench warmer. You're watching the game, all the while knowing deep down that if you were just a little bit *better*, you'd already be on the field. Married to the man. Promoted to the position. Pregnant with the baby. It's taken a painful journey for God to teach me that waiting on Him, *is* playing the game. And as such, it requires phenomenal endurance, strength, and training.

Training me to wait in a God-honoring way began with an honest look into *why* I hate waiting so much. I came up with three reasons.

I WANT CONTROL OVER MY LIFE.
I have sugar-coated this for a long time by simply describing myself as a "go-getter." I like to have a plan, and I like to accomplish it. In fact, at random times in the day, my three-year-old will point one pudgy finger forward and command, "Let's keep moving!" *(I wonder who she learned that from?)*

Moving forward gives me the illusion that I am in control of my life. Being at a God-ordained standstill when I want to be moving forward shatters that illusion. I feel like a cartoon character running as fast as I can, with somebody's hand pressed against my forehead. It doesn't matter how much I want it, I'm not going anywhere.

But oh, the sweet grace of being stopped by the hand of God! Of being reminded that He is in control. The truth is, deep down I don't want to be in control of my own life because deep down I know how inept I really am. To sit back and submit, to quit trying so hard and simply *wait* on the Trustworthy One, now that is freeing indeed! To embrace a season of waiting is to embrace the authority of God, to willingly acknowledge that He is in complete control. And it's impossible to do that and not come to a place of greater peace.

THE ACT OF WAITING IS USUALLY ACCOMPANIED BY A HOST OF LIES.
For me, it typically begins with worldly idols. For instance, I want the success and acclaim of being married to a man with a phenomenal ministry. This idol becomes enshrined in worldly thinking. *Look at that other couple—they've got it all together. Look at how their ministry is growing. If only I could have this or that, surely I'd be content.* Following the really destructive lies come the really depressing lies. *Maybe I'm just not good enough. Maybe God doesn't love me as much as He loves them. Maybe there really isn't a plan for my life.*

In order to embrace waiting, we must first win the battle for our minds. And this is no easy task! As often as the lies come—a million times a day—we must be ready to speak the truth to ourselves. Like the athlete in I Corinthians 9:24-26 who runs to win a prize, disciplining his body and forcing it to submit, we train our minds to feast off of the truth. For me, this began with memorizing Scripture that directly countered the lies I believed.

I HAD A WRONG PERSPECTIVE OF WAITING.

Earlier, I mentioned my "bench-warmer" mentality, but actually my wrong perspective went even deeper. My focus in "waiting" has always been very literal. *I am waiting to be done with school. I am waiting to meet the right guy. I am waiting to get a job.* You get the idea. But the Bible makes it clear that the thing we are to be waiting for is the Lord Himself:

> I wait for the Lord, my soul waits,
> and in his word I hope;
> my soul waits for the Lord
> more than the watchmen for the morning,
> more than watchmen for the morning.[57]

You see, we aren't just waiting to pass the home study, make it through medical school, enter remission, or celebrate a family member's conversion. We're waiting for God Himself—His presence to fill us, to make us more like Him, to take us deeper into the heart of who He is. And amazingly, how does He do this? *By allowing us to wait.* The very act of waiting is sanctifying in and of itself! And in this, we can take great heart. If you, like me, are in a season of waiting, allow me to say I know how hard it is. Believe me, I do. But may I encourage both of us with this glorious truth—you and I *are* moving forward... just not outwardly. We are moving forward into becoming the people He wants us to be. We are moving forward in developing patience, trust, and submission to His perfect will. We are moving forward into the very heart of God. All this waiting, it's not a break in the plan; it's part of it.

So in these seasons of waiting, let's train our minds not just to know the truth, but to believe it. Let's train our hearts to trust the heart of God with greater and greater stamina, so that if He should say to us, "Wait another month...wait another year...wait indefinitely," we might courageously and willingly respond, *"Yes, Lord!"* If we do that, we're not only out on the field; we're winning the game.

Getting Real about the Girl Behind the Grin

Sometimes I feel like a total mess. I'm not talking about day-old mascara and greasy hair. Those things may have bothered me in a distant teenage life, but now? *Please!* I'm just thankful I still *have* hair after the number of times it's been chewed, yanked, and caught in zippers. No, when I say I feel like a mess it's not on the outside. It's on the inside.

Anybody can take a hot shower, tidy the kitchen, and put on a bright smile. But beneath the smile I often feel like a frazzled storm of unfinished tasks, thinly concealed irritations, throbbing inadequacy, and weary battles to believe God. It's as if my outside and inside are disconnected:

- "Yes, sweetheart, Mommy's listening." *Say my name one more time and I'll slam my head in the dishwasher.*
- "Can I get you more manicotti?" *Good gravy, I'm going to be doing dishes 'til midnight.*
- "We're just waiting on God!" *Who I'm beginning to fear is never going to show up.*

Of course there are those moments when the inside erupts onto the outside:

- "For the love of all things sacred, give me some SPACE!"
- "COOK IT YOURSELF!"
- "I just don't feel like God loves me!" **sob, sob, sob, sob, sob*

But for the most part, I'm pretty talented when it comes to the outside. I know how to put on a cute outfit, camouflage the mess, and get the job done. And that's what scares me. Because unlike most people, Jesus has never been fooled, nor impressed by the outside. "Woe to you, scribes and Pharisees, hypocrites!" He cries in Matthew 23:27. "For you are like whitewashed tombs, which outwardly appear beautiful, but within are full of dead people's bones and all uncleanness."

How's that for a metaphor? So what do we do when our whitewashed exterior is as thin as a coat of nail polish and our interior is daily filling with decay?

Dear sister, we limp back to the cross.

The cross reminds us that life was not always this way. That once, long ago, there was no outside/inside disconnect. Once, all the joy and perfection we pretend to have on Facebook was truly felt in our souls. Mankind was at peace with God, with one another, and with self. Then sin entered the picture and just like that, all of creation *broke.* Nature, animals, mankind—together we began to *groan* under the weight of our own brokenness.[58] And nothing could remedy the problem. Not outward appearances. Not religious practices. Not cute guys, or big homes, or double-stuffed Oreos. Nothing, except the cross. When Jesus died on the cross He absorbed the full weight of sin—the penalty, wrath, bondage, and brokenness. And He rose victorious. That single act has the power to obliterate the outside/inside disconnect.

In his book *Jesus + Nothing = Everything,* Tullian Tchividjian recounts a difficult season in his life. He writes:

> Rediscovering the gospel enabled me to see that: because Jesus was strong for me, I was free to be weak. Because Jesus won for me, I was free to lose. Because Jesus was someone, I was free to be no one. Because Jesus was extraordinary, I was free to be ordinary. Because Jesus succeeded for me, I was free to fail.[59]

You and I don't have to pretend we've got it all together on the outside. We need only draw near to Him by faith and in His sufficiency find our rest.

Is There Such a Thing as Calling?

A friend asked me this question several months ago. In context, I knew she wasn't referring to a "general" or "primary" calling to live for Christ. She was asking me if I believe there is such a thing as a "specific" or "secondary" calling, like the calling to become a doctor or a missionary.

I understood the question because people talk about this sort of "calling" all the time. They say things like, "I just felt *called* to do it." Called to marry him. Called to plant a church. Called to adopt. Called to give. Some people love to talk about calling so much that you wonder if they go to the grocery store and feel "called" to buy Crest toothpaste instead of Colgate. These kind of people used to frustrate me. It felt like they had a private line with God, and He just told them everything to do, say, think, eat, and moisturize with. To be honest, I was jealous. Many times it felt like I begged God for discernment and heard crickets in the background. I always wanted to exclaim, *But how do you* know *you're called?*

Suffice to say, I've pondered my friend's question long before she asked it. I usually find myself thinking about calling in one of two life scenarios—either before making a major decision, or in a season of difficulty and discouragement. In the former scenario, I'm hoping not to make a mistake. In the latter, I'm wondering if I already did.

The funny thing about "calling" is it's deeply tied to our view of God. The person who is wondering about calling is the person who is secretly hoping God actually has a plan for her life. Secretly hoping she hasn't somehow fallen out of His hands. Secretly hoping He loves her enough to be intimately involved in the details of her life. I should know; I *am* that person. So do I believe there's such a thing as calling?

Yes. I believe God has a specific calling for every single person. I believe this because the God of the Bible is vastly personal, with the power to bestow wisdom, to direct our steps, and to equip us to do His will.[60] The God of the Bible is so completely *sovereign* that even the sparrows don't fall to the ground apart from His design.[61] Surely He has a will for us.

But the tricky thing is, He may not reveal it to us right now. If there is one thing I have learned from the book of Genesis, it's that **callings from God are revealed and fulfilled in His timing.** Abraham waited *twenty-five years* for God to give him Isaac. Joseph was seventeen years old when He had a vision of his brothers bowing before him, and he was *thirty-nine* years old when the vision came to pass. Clearly the presence of waiting is not the absence of calling. In fact, it might be the hallmark of it! I cannot think of a single instance in the Bible where God revealed a calling *in its entirety*, and then fulfilled it immediately.

Which brings me to the second thing I've learned about calling: **Callings from God are not free of suffering.** Look back at Joseph again. It amazes me to think that while he sat in prison, he was in the very center of God's will for his life. I would've been begging, "Surely there is a plan B! This *cannot* be your plan for my life!" But it was. It just wasn't the plan in its entirety. It was a piece of the plan. It was a dark and painful season that transformed a cocky seventeen-year-old boy into the God-fearing governor of Egypt. In other words, *there is a* *purpose for the suffering!* There is a purpose for all the waiting and all the agonizing growth. It's not a deviation from the plan; it's part of it.

In the meantime, you can plant your hope firmly in the fact that **callings from God are for His glory and our good.** All along, God loved Joseph. All along, the plan was intended to glorify God and to bless Joseph, something Joseph himself understood when he told his brothers, "As for you, you meant evil against me, but God meant it for good."[62]

Dear sister (or brother), if you belong to God, you will never fall out of His hand. You will never be big enough to thwart His will, or ruin His ability to use your life for His glory. There is always a plan. Even in the silence.

While you wait for God's *specific* calling for your life to come together, the Bible overflows with His clearly revealed *general* calling for all people. He has called us to holiness, to share the gospel of Christ, to be filled with the Spirit, to love and forgive like Christ, to rejoice always, pray without ceasing, and give thanks in all circumstances.[63] God has called us to *Himself.* To a relationship with Him, in which we become *like* Him by His own power and grace. He has called us to surrender, to be at peace with the things we do not know because we are at peace with the One who controls them.

Lest you think I am writing this from a position of great comfort and security, I am not. I am writing it from Joseph's cell, from that place of quiet and painful patience. But the more I do what Joseph did—embracing the season, serving the cupbearer and the baker and working with all my heart as unto the Lord—the more I see that this is a place of great freedom. This is the place where fear flees, because it is the place where you finally believe that nothing can separate you from the love of Christ. It is the place where character deepens, faith blossoms, and hope overcomes. It is the very center of God's will.

When Life Disappoints

I wanted security, and You gave me chaos,
Wanted esteem, and You let me know shame.
I wanted success, and You handed me failure,
Wanted Your pleasure, and experienced Your pain.

I wanted simplicity, and You gave me troubles,
Wanted grandeur, and was reduced to nothing.
I wanted approval, and You handed me rejection,
Wanted Your blessing, and tasted Your suffering.

So I packed my frustration, and all my complaints
Into two giant burlap sacks,
And one I named "Bitterness" and the other "Disappointment,"
And heaved them upon my back.

Thus I began my journey to You,
Because I needed an answer, you see,
For all of the things You'd promised me once,
And failed to deliver to me.

But the loads, they grew heavy with each passing day,
Til I fumed with fury and hate;
And I moaned and I wept and I stumbled at last
Beneath their unbearable weight.

I looked at these bags, laden with trials,
And deep in my soul I knew,
That I could not carry, nor change, nor fight them;
There was but one thing left to do.

I reached both arms, fierce as I dared,
And I hugged them to my breast,
Then I heaved and hauled and wrenched until,
I'd wrestled them into my chest.

I cried to the heavens, "I embrace these trials!
I welcome them full unto me,
Let them now work Your will in my life
So that I may be more like Thee!"

The trials spilled over, into my lap
Each of them laid before me,
And as I sat and stared anew,
Suddenly I saw them most clearly.

I wanted comfort, and You gave me character,
Wanted completion, and You gave me patience.
I wanted glory, and You gave me humility,
Wanted Your promise, and You gave me Your presence.

I wanted ease, and You gave me strength,
Wanted cheap idols, and You offered me wealth,
I wanted garbage, and You gave me riches,
Wanted your gifts, and You gave me Yourself.

I laughed and I danced and I started to sing,
For the treasures I held in my lap!
Then I looked back and forth and finally found
My two giant burlap sacks.

And the names on the bags were re-written,
For God had seen fit to destroy
Both "Bitterness" and "Disappointment,"
And to name them "Steadfastness" and "Joy."

I fell to my knees and worshiped and cried,
"Oh God, all along You knew,
That deep in my heart from the very beginning,
All I really wanted was You."

An Ode to My Twenties

Dear Twenties,

Today I am thirty years old. As I close this book, I also close a chapter of my life—ten sweet years with you. I'll have you know I've liked you a lot more than the teens. You are the decade that got rid of acne, gave me a job that didn't come with an apron, and taught me how to spread my wings and fly away from home. You introduced me to love, turned me into a bride, and washed away the insecurities of adolescence with the affection of a man I never deserved.

You are the decade of burnt dinners, tiny apartments, and tender beginnings. The decade that laid a little body into my arms and in one swift moment made me a mother for life. Where adolescence taught me to be strong because I have not, you taught me to be strong because I *have.* You tutored me with kindness. With blessings that made me ache to be better than I am. No matter what the future brings, I will remember you as the decade that gave me the gifts that would come to define my life and my legacy.

My dear twenties, you have been merciful to me. A decade of joy, lavished with grace. I used to view you as the ticking-clock decade, the race-to-the-deadline decade. But I know better now. Your goal has never been for me to gather accomplishments and pin them to my chest before I'm thirty. Because you are not the finish line, but the starting line. If childhood and adolescence are the "Ready" and "Set," you are the gunshot decade that gives us a swift kick in the pants and tells us to "Go!" Take your life and your blessings, and live! Put wings to your dreams, and courage to your feet, and don't be so afraid to stumble along the way. *Thank you,* dear twenties. I will always cherish you.

Endnotes

1. Eccles. 5:18 ESV
2. Paul David Tripp, *What did you Expect?* (Wheaton, Illinois: Crossway, 2010), 75.
3. Ibid., 43-53.
4. Sally Lloyd-Jones, *The Jesus Storybook Bible* (Grand Rapids, Michigan: Zondervan, 2007), 242.
5. Eph. 6:4, Acts 17:24-27 ESV
6. Isa. 8:13 NASB
7. Kevin DeYoung, *Crazy Busy* (Illinois: Crossway, 2013), Kindle edition.
8. Luke 15 ESV
9. CJ Mahaney, *Humility* (Colorado: Multnomah Books, 2005), 160-161.
10. Rom. 3:10, 23 ESV
11. Prov. 13:25 NIV
12. Eph. 6:1-3, Exod. 20:12, 1 Tim. 3:4-5 ESV
13. Eph. 6:10, Matt. 11:28-30 ESV
14. Ps. 103:19, 139:16; 2 Cor. 5:10 ESV
15. 1 Cor. 1:27-31 ESV
16. Paul David Tripp, *Dangerous Calling* (Illinois: Crossway, 2012), 21.
17. Ps. 46:1-2 NIV
18. Ps. 139:16 ESV
19. Ps. 27:1, 4 NIV
20. Prov. 19:18, 22:6, 23:19; Eph. 6:4 ESV
21. Rom. 5:6-8, 2 Pet. 3:9, Isa. 61:1-3, 2 Cor. 5:17 ESV
22. Gen. 24:67 NIV
23. 1 Pet. 1:3-4 ESV
24. Os Guinness, *The Call* (Nashville, Tennessee: W Publishing Group, 2003), 190.

[25] Brother Lawrence, *The Practice of the Presence of God* (Massachusetts: New Seeds Books, 2005).

[26] Sally Lloyd-Jones, *The Jesus Storybook Bible* (Grand Rapids, Michigan: Zondervan, 2007), 25.

[27] Mindy Starns Clark, *The House That Cleans Itself* (Oregon: Harvest House Publishers, 2007).

[28] 1 Cor. 6:19, Rom. 12:1 ESV

[29] James 4:6, Matt. 7:1 ESV

[30] Ps. 46:1, 91:2; 2 Cor. 1:3-5 ESV

[31] Matt. 11:29 ESV

[32] 1 Pet. 2:9 NIV

[33] 2 Cor. 12:9 NIV

[34] Gal. 2:20, paraphrased

[35] 1 Cor. 9:24-27 ESV

[36] Luke 10:38-42, John 4:1-30, Joshua 2, Matt. 9:20-22, John 19 ESV

[37] Paul David Tripp, *What did you Expect?* (Illinois: Crossway, 2010), 58.

[38] John 16:33 NIV

[39] 1 Pet. 3:1-5 ESV

[40] Isa. 14:14 NIV

[41] http://www.merriam-webster.com/dictionary/submit

[42] Phil. 2:2-8 ESV

[43] Matt. 16:25, Rom. 6:22 ESV

[44] Wayne Grudem, *Evangelical Feminism* (Illinois: Crossway Books, 2006), 261-263.

[45] Lauren Bradshaw. "12 Things We Learned about Love in 2012," *Redbook,* December 2012. Accessed February 22, 2015. http://www.redbookmag.com/love-sex/relationships/advice/g1362/best-love-stories-of-2012/

[46] Ps. 18:16-17 ESV

[47] Eph. 1:3-11 ESV

[48] 1 Cor. 1:25 ESV

49 Ps. 131:2 ESV

50 Titus 2:3-5, Eph. 5:22-24, Prov. 31, 1 Pet. 3:1-6 ESV

51 Hosea 11:8 NASB

52 Hannah Hurnard, *Hinds Feet on High Places* (London: The Olive Press, 1955), 63.

53 Ibid., 218.

54 Ibid., 176.

55 2 Cor. 5:17, John 1:12, Ps. 139, Gal. 1:10 ESV

56 Ps. 25:15 ESV

57 Ps. 130:5-6 NASB

58 Rom. 8:22 ESV

59 Tullian Tchividjian, *Jesus + Nothing = Everything* (Illinois: Crossway, 2011), 24.

60 James 1:5, Prov. 16:9, Heb. 13:21 ESV

61 Matt. 10:29 ESV

62 Gen. 50:20 NASB

63 1 Thess. 4:7, 5:15-18; Matt. 28:18-20; Eph. 5:18, 4:32 ESV